PORSCHE

Peter Morgan

Photography by John Colley

motorbooks

First published in 2012 by MBI Publishing Company and Motorbooks, an imprint of Quarto Publishing Group USA Inc., 400 First Avenue North, Suite 400, Minneapolis, MN 55401 USA

Motorbooks titles are also available at discounts in bulk quantity for industrial or sales-promotional use. For details write to Special Sales Manager at Quarto Publishing Group USA Inc., 400 First Avenue North, Suite 400, Minneapolis, MN 55401 USA.

To find out more about our books, visit us online at www.motorbooks.com.

Library of Congress Cataloging-in-Publication Data
Morgan, Peter, 1951 Dec. 14–
  Porsche / Peter Morgan ; photographs, John Colley. – 1st ed.
    p. cm.
Includes index.
ISBN 978-0-7603-4261-9 (softbound with flaps)
1. Porsche automobiles—History. 2. Colley, John.   I. Title.
TL215.P75M6696 2012
629.222—dc23
2011043497

CEO: Ken Fund
Publisher: Zack Miller
Editor: Jordan Wiklund
Design Manager: Brad Springer
Layout: Kazuko Collins
Cover designer: Matthew Simmons

Printed in China

10 9 8 7 6 5 4 3

On the front cover: 2012 911 Carrera S
On the frontis: 804 F1
On the title page: 911 Carrera (997)
On the back cover: 1965 911, 1996 Boxster, 2009 Cayenne S Hybrid

CONTENTS

Today, the name of Porsche is known worldwide as a manufacturer of the very best sports cars. Porsche is also accepted as a benchmark for leading-edge automotive technology and, of course, its successes on the racetracks of the world gild a brand image that is the envy of other manufacturers. It is a reputation that has taken many decades to develop.

The story of Porsche is remarkable because it contains so much drama. There have been family feuds, times when the company balanced on the brink of bankruptcy, and times when it seemed that nothing was impossible in the world of both automobile manufacture and motorsport. The hand-to-mouth existence in the early years will include no surprises to anybody who runs their own business and experienced the agony and ecstasy of seeing their company grow. Indeed, what the Porsches went through in the mid-1940s demonstrates how close one's family is to the heart of any personal enterprise. The key asset that the company had in those early years was an experienced and loyal staff who clearly went the extra mile for their employer. The reality was that there was little else going for them in what was a wrecked Europe. But we see those factors of talent and loyalty emerging all the way through the subsequent Porsche story—of brilliant minds and unswerving loyalty delivering the unexpected—regularly.

The man who established this remarkable culture was Ferry Porsche. He didn't have the fiery, engineering genius of his famous father, but he made up for it in having a rare ability to take his people with him into corners of the engineering envelope that many would consider impossible. He bred a unique atmosphere of loyalty within Porsche and became a role model through his quiet, respectful manner and absolutely clear vision of where he wanted his company to be.

It is no coincidence that brilliant minds gathered around Ferry. He didn't have to search them out; they came to him. And as they worked, it was a thrill for them to be able to talk to Ferry about what they were doing and get his valuable guidance. Some might say Ferry was a good manager, but the reality is that history will say he was a great leader.

No story of Porsche can exclude the story of its most famous model, the 911. On publication

of this book, the 911 will have celebrated its 50th birthday. The continuing ability of generations of Porsche engineers to reinterpret the sports car philosophy conceived by Ferry Porsche and so brilliantly delivered in 1963 is almost unbelievable. It simply doesn't make sense that in a market that is so famously fickle, demanding, and competitive, one model can survive at the top for so long. But it has, and shows no sign of stepping down as the automobile industry tentatively takes its first steps into the post-petroleum-fueled era.

In this book we follow the cars that have made Porsche the great automobile manufacturer it is today. The satisfying aspect of writing about this heritage is knowing that the story is far from over. We can only wonder what records, achievements, and inventions the Porsche engineers of the future will deliver.

CHAPTER 1

FIRST STEPS

Ferdinand Porsche established his automotive design consultancy in 1931. By this time he was recognized as a brilliant automotive engineer who had risen to head of engineering at Daimler Benz in the 1920s. He established his consultancy in a suburb of Stuttgart, Germany, called Zuffenhausen, and in the late 1930s achieved world recognition for his designs of the Auto Union grand prix machine and for a very low cost People's Car—the car that would later become known across the world as the Volkswagen Beetle.

His son Ferry was born in 1909 and grew up surrounded by a culture devoted to cars and race car development. Working beside his father, Ferry developed a thorough understanding of the requirements not only of street cars, but also race cars.

In 1944, to escape the heavy allied bombing, the core members of the Porsche company moved to the remote village of Gmünd, deep in the Carpathian mountains in southwestern Austria. It was here in the early post-war years, and while his father was interned, that Ferry found his feet as a business leader, keeping the company alive by constructing farm equipment, repairing the military vehicles of the allied occupation forces, and working out of a collection of timber huts that had once been used as a sawmill. Nevertheless, the treasure that was within this tiny company was its huge experience—which dated back to before the consultancy's beginnings in the early 1930s.

From late 1945, the main priority was to secure the release of the interned Ferdinand Porsche. Imprisoned by the French in 1945 after allegations that he was involved in war crimes, Porsche was imprisoned in Dijon and released in 1947 after the charges were dropped. In the end this came down to a fairly sordid payment of money. The "bail money"

was paid using the proceeds of a design contract that good fortune and an undoubted hunger for work had placed in their hands. The Porsches had many friends in mainland Europe, not least by virtue of the reputation created by the Auto Union GP cars. Italian industrialist Piero Dusio had a dream to build a grand prix car and a new sports car, and he turned to the fledgling Porsche company to help him build it.

The Cisitalia contract would be the making of the company. The 1947 GP car featured all-wheel drive transmission for its mid-mounted double overhead camshaft, 12-cylinder supercharged engine. The water-cooled horizontally opposed engine produced no less than 385 horsepower from just 1.5 liters of displacement. In the austere and extremely constrained post-war economic climate in Europe, it was a masterpiece of resourcefulness and innovation. Unfortunately, however, the sponsor ran out of money and the car never raced, but the little Porsche company had put down a marker of its capabilities, and thoughts in Gmünd turned to producing their own sports car. Within a year, the nearby Katschberg mountain passes were echoing to the sounds of small, two-seat sports cars being put through their paces.

The story of Porsche as a car manufacturer had begun.

The inspiration and motivation for Porsche to build a sports car came from the fact that from 1946, examples of Ferdinand Porsche's Volkswagen Beetle had begun to roll off the purpose-built factory production line at the new factory in Wolfsburg, Germany. Ferry Porsche and his hugely experienced chief engineer Karl Rabe realized they could use the mechanical components of the Beetle for a new two-seat sports car. The Beetle's mechanical components should have dictated a rear engine layout for the engine and gearbox, but this wasn't the ideal layout for an agile sports car. The engineers followed their work on the earlier Cisitalia by making the first car to carry the Porsche name mid-engined. This layout gave the mere 1290-lb

(585 kg) prototype a near ideal front/back weight distribution—perfect for handling the car around fast bends. It was a relatively easy job to mount the engine ahead of the transmission to the rear wheels rather than behind as on the Beetle. From the start the car was built with light weight and high speed in mind and featured a beautifully aerodynamic, hand-beaten aluminium sheet body mounted on a pressed steel chassis.

By March 1948, there were bodyless prototypes running around the local villages and over the nearby mountain passes as Porsche's engineers put the new car through a rigorous testing process. The car was certified for street use three months later.

This first Porsche used the Beetle's independent suspension (including torsion bars at the rear) and cable-operated drum brakes. The mildly tuned, flat-4 air-cooled engine developed just 35 horsepower from its 1100cc, but thanks to its wind-cheating aerodynamic profile it could run nearly 85 mph—much faster than most street cars of the day anywhere in Europe.

PORSCHE #1

Engine: Air-cooled flat 4-cylinder, mid-mounted with single camshaft and two pushrod-operated valves for each cylinder. Single downdraft carburetor.
Displacement: 1,131 cc
Output: 35 horsepower (26kW) at 4,000 rpm
Gearbox: 4-speed manual
Chassis: Mid-engine, rear wheel drive, steel ladder frame on two-seat aluminium bodyshell
Performance: Maximum speed: 84 mph; 0–62 mph in 23 seconds

Did You Know?

It took just one year to turn Porsche No. 1 from a concept into a usable sports car. It was the product of just a handful of highly motivated design engineers working out of a small timber cabin with a few old drawing boards, a telephone, and a coal-burning stove for equipment.

Even as Porsche No. 1 began its testing in March 1948, coupe and cabriolet versions of the 356 were being prepared in the tiny design office in Gmünd, Austria. No. 1 had been a prototype using a rigid, but space-hungry, steel ladder frame. With the car's mid-engine layout, there was also no space for luggage. For their production car designs, the engineers fell back on the original Beetle layout, placing the engine behind the rear axle and using a pressed steel floorpan (with notable box sections at the side for stiffness) to gain more interior space, including rear emergency seats or space for luggage. In most other respects, the mechanical components were taken straight from the contemporary Volkswagen Beetle. The first "production" 356 was registered in July 1948, and within six months, regular

production commenced at the rate of five cars every month (both coupes and cabriolets). The notable feature of these first Gmünd cars was that each still had a hand-crafted aerodynamic aluminium body, but this helped give the early cars a weight of just 1,700 lb (780 kg).

Demand for the 356 sports cars was immediately brisk, and after two years production was transferred back to Porsche's larger premises in Zuffenhausen, Stuttgart. With many changes to make the car easier to build, including a pressed steel body, 356 production accelerated rapidly once German production was underway.

The original 1,100cc engine began with 40 horsepower, but a 1,300cc version came in 1951 and was soon followed by a 1,500 producing 60 horsepower. A 1500S unit later produced 70 horsepower. By 1955, there were only 1300 and 1500 engines and a revised 356A version. In 1957, the first Carrera model was introduced with the 100-horsepower "Fuhrmann" four-cam engine. Two years later came the 356B, with the model evolving into a refined touring sports car and a long way from the simple VW-based Gmünd models of 10 years earlier. The 356C arrived in 1963 and by the time 356 production ended in 1965, some 76,000 cars had been manufactured.

PORSCHE 356 (1300S, 1954-55)

Engine: Air-cooled flat 4-cylinder, pushrod-operated single camshaft
Displacement: 1,290cc
Output: 60 horsepower at 5,500 rpm
Gearbox: 4-speed manual
Chassis: Rear engine, rear wheel drive, unitary construction steel 2+2 bodyshell
Performance: Maximum speed: 99 mph; 0–62 mph in 17 seconds

Did You Know?

The Porsche crest was introduced on the steering hub of the 356 in 1953. The crest was a combination of the coats of arms of Stuttgart and the region of Württemburg, with the Porsche name at the top.

The immediate success of the first 356s in motorsport fueled a demand for even more sporting versions, particularly from the United States. By 1952, Porsche tested the saleability of its cars for motorsport more directly with a limited edition of around 15 America Roadsters. This was loosely a street model, using the steel structure of the Cabriolet with a lightweight, aluminium body, but it was the first Porsche designed with competition in mind. The very basic Roadster was given the 70-horsepower 1500S 4-cylinder engine, and the cars proved to be very popular for U.S. national racing and boosted interest in the new German sports car maker. But by the mid-1950s, it was clear the American market was ready for a more widely available sports-focused street machine. Using the experience of the America Roadster, the Speedster was more manufacturable, being based again on the Cabriolet but with a steel bodyshell and steeply raked wrap-around windshield.

The Speedster was a stunning car to look at and yelled "speed" from every angle. It was also very basically equipped and, as a result, light. It featured minimal weather equipment and lightweight bucket seats (featuring two slots in the squab and high sides for support). The simple canvas roof seriously cut down headroom, and with the plastic sidescreens fitted, visibility all around was hopeless. This was a car you drove with the top down. There was no room for anybody in the back seats and even the dash panel was redesigned to carry just two big dials (speedometer and engine rev counter) and a smaller oil temperature dial. At 1750 lbs (794 kg) it was around 150 lbs lighter than the production 356 and was available with the 55 horsepower and 70 horsepower 1500 engines. Initially, the Speedster was intended to only be sold in the United States, but it wasn't long before the car was on sale worldwide.

The whole character of the Speedster was "racing car for the road," and while the concept didn't appeal to every type of sports car driver, it put the Porsche name on motorsport results sheets across the world.

PORSCHE 356A SPEEDSTER SUPER (1954-58)

Engine: Air-cooled flat 4-cylinder, pushrod-operated overhead valves

Displacement: 1582 cc

Output: 75 horsepower (51kW) at 5000 rpm

Gearbox: 4-speed manual

Chassis: Rear-engine, rear wheel drive, unitary construction steel 2+2 bodyshell

Performance: Maximum speed: 109 mph; 0–62 mph in 14.5 seconds

Did You Know?

The Speedster was the first Porsche to feature rubber-edged bright trim on the rocker panels and chromed hub caps—features that would quickly be added to the other Porsche models.

CHAPTER 2

EARLY RACE CARS

Racing is in the DNA of Porsche. When Ferdinand Porsche began designing and building cars for his employers at the beginning of the twentieth century, there was always a will to show their performance in the heat of competition. In the 1920s and 1930s, the old professor produced some landmark racing cars, including the Mercedes SSK and the remarkable V-16 rear-engined Auto Union grand prix car. After the end of the Second World War, it was left to his son Ferry to pick up the pieces of the Porsche consultancy business, and that first project for Piero Dusio gave the automotive world a wake-up call that Porsche was back in the race business.

After the first 356 emerged from Gmünd and was sold to an enthusiastic Swiss customer, it was almost immediately put to the test in competition. Word spread quickly and Porsche was soon present in motorsport events of all kinds across Western Europe.

It was the French importer Auguste Veuillet who suggested running a car in the 1951 Le Mans 24 Hour endurance race. This was no small undertaking for Porsche, as there was still a lot of anti-German sentiment in the French regional capital. Nevertheless, Veuillet persuaded Ferry Porsche that it would be a good idea to increase the awareness of the new cars. The Veuillet/Mouche Gmund 356 coupe, its 1086cc engine developing all of 46 horsepower, won its class and finished 20th overall, beginning a tradition of Porsche competing at Le Mans that has continued unbroken every year since.

It went without saying that the original 1100cc VW-based engine was being tuned significantly for these competitions. Progressively, the VW parts were being replaced by special Porsche-designed and -made parts to increase capacity and power. As more 356s emerged from the Zuffenhausen factory, more of them traveled worldwide, spreading the word of Porsche performance. In particular, the cars found a popular niche in the United States, where they were frequently modified for both club and national-level events. The America Roadster was the first step toward a pure competition Porsche, and the Speedster soon followed. With its 1500cc motor, it was the perfect weapon for the amateur driver.

Meanwhile, the experience of Le Mans and other top-level competitions had indicated that a more dedicated race car (and engine) was required if Porsche was to show how good its cars could be. It was a measure of Ferry Porsche that he always instructed his engineers that racing should be used to improve the production cars, and that Porsche's customers should be excited by the racing-derived spin-offs that were a feature of the street cars.

One of Porsche's earliest German dealers, Walter Glöckler, was the first to experiment with a purpose-built race car using Porsche components, the engine being fitted to a light tubular chassis and clothed in a minimalist spyder (roadster) body. The weight savings were significant, the Glöckler-Porsche tipping the scales at just 986 lbs (450 kg), with a methanol-fueled engine producing 98 horsepower. A second car was timed at no less than 133 mph.

The message was not lost on Ferry Porsche, and over the winter of 1952-53, his engineers set to work designing a brand-new ladder-frame-race car with a lightweight aluminium body. The type 550 would be Porsche's first race car—the first of many that would follow in future years and decades.

A team of two 550 race cars was entered for the 1953 Le Mans 24 Hours. These cars featured uninsulated aluminium hardtops that helped give them a top speed of around 125 mph on the long Le Mans straights. The drivers were heroes, not least because the unheated cockpits were very cold during the night hours and the noise levels would be considered unbearable today. The cars were powered by the 75 horsepower 1500S pushrod 4-cylinder,

1955 550-1500RS SPYDER

Engine: 547 air-cooled flat 4-cylinder, 4 camshafts
Displacement: 1498 cc
Output: 125 horsepower (92kW) at 6500 rpm
Gearbox: 718 5-speed manual
Chassis: Two-seat steel ladder-frame chassis with aluminium body panels
Performance: Maximum speed 122 mph

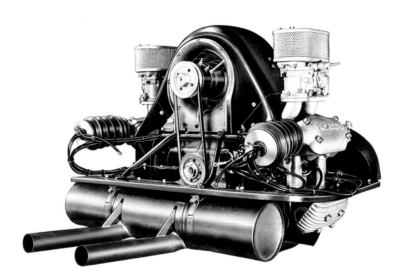

550 SPYDER

Did You Know?

The name "Spyder" derives from the exotic
naming of the American two-seater roadsters
from the likes of Stutz, Cord, and Duesenberg
in the 1920s. It is said the word derives from
the insect spider, which was the description
given in the 1800s for a light, 4-wheeled
horse-drawn carriage called a Tilbury-
Phaeton. With large rear and smaller front
wheels, combined with a lightweight folding
top, it looked like a spider.

and impressive reliability enabled both cars to dead-heat for first-in-class after a day's racing. It was the first of many successes for the 550. Later that year, one of the same 550s won its class in the grueling Carrera Panamericana road race in Mexico (right).

For the 1954 season, Porsche entered a works team of the new cars and called them the 550 1500RS. The 1500RS featured a brand-new 4-camshaft engine (the 547) designed largely by a young Porsche engineer named Ernst Fuhrmann. The 110-horsepower "4-cam" would turn the 550 into a regular class winner worldwide. In Europe, drivers Hans Herrmann and Herbert Linge finished sixth overall in the famous Mille Miglia 1000-mile road race around Italy. A works entry in the 1954 Carrera Panamericana delivered an incredible third overall for Hans Herrmann. From this point, Porsche insiders began to refer to the 4-cam as the "Carrera" engine—a tag that stuck and later came into use for Porsche's faster car models.

Private owners would build the legend that has become the 550 Spyder, and it wasn't all based on winning races. American 1950s movie star James Dean was killed driving his 550 Spyder in a road accident in California (on the way to a race meeting), while in Europe, Porsche factory driver Richard von Frankenberg made headlines when his streamlined 550 flew off the banking at the famed Avus raceway in Berlin.

For 1956, a new version of the 550 was evolved with a stiffer chassis and a further developed 4-cam engine producing 130 horsepower. The icing on the cake for the 550A was Umberto Maglioli's overall win on the Targa Florio road race in Sicily.

The British manufacturers Lotus and Cooper kept Porsche honest in the mid-1950s, and their continuous innovation began to reveal basic shortfalls in the 550A's specification. First run in 1957, the 718RSK was an entirely new approach to race car design by Porsche. The design carried over the Mercedes-Benz–derived "low pivot" rear swing axle design, but the front suspension moved away from

1959 718RSK

Engine: Air-cooled flat 4-cylinder, gear-driven double overhead camshafts
Displacement: 1498 cc
Output: 160 horsepower at 7600 rpm
Gearbox: 5-speed manual
Chassis: Mid engine, rear wheel drive, tubular space-frame with aluminium body
Performance: Maximum speed 155–165 mph

the Beetle arrangement to a new twin trailing arm system operating laminated torsion bars. The chassis was now a full multi-tubular steel spaceframe with a more aerodynamic aluminium body. Facing fierce competition, the RSK developed rapidly, and both suspension and engine improved significantly. By 1959, the 1.5-liter "Fuhrmann" 4-cam was producing 140 horsepower, with reliability to run endurance races as well as sprints. The British cars tended to be lighter and nimbler, but the speed of the RSK was undisputed—factory driver Richard von Frankenberg achieved 160 mph in a special 1600cc car in 1958.

In fact, Porsche's team of star drivers—Jean Behra, Paul Frère, Hans Herrmann, and Edgar Barth—really put the little Porsches on the racing map. After a 3–4–5 finish at Le Mans

Did You Know?
The "K" in RSK comes from the shape of the chassis tubes supporting the front suspension torsion bars, which sloped down from the top outer pivots to join at the centerline of the car.

in 1958, Jo Bonnier and Wolfgang von Trips drove an RSK to third at Sebring in 1959 behind the far more powerful Ferraris. At the Sicilian Targa Florio race that year, the RSK won the first overall victory for Porsche in a world championship event. In 1960, the RSK was changed only in detail, but was called the RS60—the cars won overall at Sebring and again on the Targa Florio. It was the RSK's speed at the daunting Reims course in France that prompted Porsche to try first Formula 2 and subsequently F1. In endurance racing, the RS60 evolved into the RS61 the following year, and eventually into the much-loved W-RS Spyder—this latter car using the 210 horsepower 8-cylinder derived from the 1962 F1 engine. Edgar Barth took his third European Hillclimb Championship in a W-RS Spyder in 1964, rounding off a remarkable seven years at the top of international sports car racing.

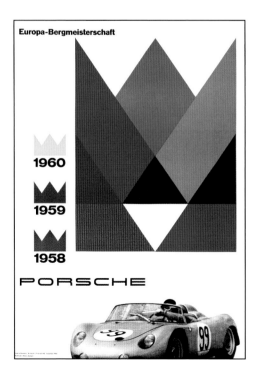

The 550 Spyder's success showed Porsche that it could be very competitive in international motorsport. Porsche had the durability for long-distance events and it had the speed thanks to the always impressive 4-cam engine. And by 1958, the 718 RSK provided the chassis to regularly beat the class competition and often embarrass the larger capacity cars.

The factory soon realized that an only slightly modified RSK could be competitive in the contemporary Formula Two, the open-wheel class just below Formula One. For the next two

years, Porsche competed successfully in F2 and eventually graduated to F1 with ever more powerful single-seat versions of the RSK. The success was addictive, and when the F1 rules changed to limit engine capacity to 1500cc for 1961, Porsche produced a brand-new F1 car.

The 804 was a slim, spaceframe car that featured an all-new horizontally opposed 8-cylinder air-cooled engine (below). Effectively, it used all the knowledge gained from the Fuhrmann 4-cam, so it should have been impressive from its first tests in early 1961.

1962 804 F1

Engine: 753 air-cooled, flat 8-cylinder, fuel injection with 2 valves per cylinder
Displacement: 1494 cc
Output: 180 horsepower (132kW) at 9200rpm
Gearbox: 6-speed manual
Chassis: Mid-engine with steel tubular spaceframe single-seat chassis
Performance: Maximum speed 170 mph

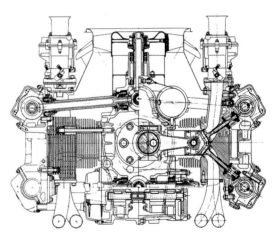

Did You Know?

Dan Gurney's French Grand Prix win in 1962 remains the only ever championship Grand Prix victory taken by a car bearing the Porsche name.

Unfortunately, maximum power was well below expectations and not enough to take on the British Coventry Climax 4-cylinder or the jewel-like Ferrari V-6. While the F1 team continued to run the RSK-derived 4-cylinder cars in 1961, work continued on the 8-cylinder.

The 804 made its grand prix debut at the 1962 Dutch Grand Prix, but the 8-cylinder was still only producing around 180 horsepower (132kW), some 20 horsepower (15kW) short of the impressive Ferraris. It didn't help that in the very same event, Lotus debuted their new 25, a super lightweight machine using an aluminium monocoque. Overnight, the new Lotus made all the others look like antiques. In the first few races, Porsche struggled and Ferry Porsche insisted the team take a timeout to make the car more competitive. His patience was rewarded—at the French GP, American driver Dan Gurney took the 804 to its first and only championship grand prix victory. Nonetheless, the reality was that it was a fortunate win, and despite a strong showing in the German GP and another win in the non-championship Solitude GP, the F1 program, and the 804, was stopped at the end of that season.

The 904 is unique in that it is the only machine in Porsche history to feature an all-fiberglass bodyshell that is bonded to a fabricated, box section steel chassis. The construction is (and unusually for Porsche) very novel. And for one glorious season—1964—it was the car to beat. By this time, a new Grand Touring category of sports cars required a build of at least 100 cars. Porsche had accepted that its spaceframe RSK concept wasn't suited to production in these numbers. Fiberglass was a revolutionary construction material at the time—the forerunner of the plastic composites that have become the standard for lightweight, superstrength materials used in aircraft and race car design. In 1963, Porsche's choice may have taken its inspiration from the methods used by Lotus, who were pioneers in the use of fiberglass for car bodyshells.

What really makes the 904 stand out are its gorgeous looks, penned in 1963 by a youthful Ferdinand Alexander Porsche—Ferry Porsche's eldest son—as a reprise to his work on the new Porsche production car, the 901. The engine for the new car was planned to be a race version of the new 901's 6-cylinder engine. This plan derailed when the 6-cylinder engine couldn't be ready for the first 100 904s that were built during the winter of 1963–64. The 185 horsepower (136kW) Carrera 4-cam was pressed back into service and in this form all the initial production deliveries were made. Nevertheless, during 1964, both the F1-derived 8-cylinder and the 901's 6-cylinder sports engines were evaluated in the car.

Success in competition was immediate, with the team of American drivers Briggs Cunningham/Lake Underwood winning the 2-liter class at the 1964 Sebring 12 Hours, followed by Colin Davis/Antonio Pucci winning overall on the Targa Florio. Unfortunately as ever in racing, the competition

Zum 5. Mal
Gesamtsieger

TARGA FLORIO
1964

Gesamtklassement	1. PORSCHE Carrera GTS/904	Barone Pucci/C. Davis
und GRAN TURISMO:	2. PORSCHE Carrera GTS/904	H. Linge/G. Balzarini
	7. PORSCHE Carrera GT/2 ltr.	G. Klass/J. Neerpasch
Prototypen:	1. PORSCHE Carrera GTS/8 Zyl.	E. Barth/U. Maglioli

BP Dunlop Bosch

PORSCHE

1964 904

Engine: 587 air-cooled, 4-camshaft, flat 4-cylinder
Displacement: 1966cc
Output: 185 horsepower (136 kW) at 7200 rpm
Gearbox: 5-speed manual
Chassis: Twin longitudinal steel box sections with integral fiberglass coupe bodyshell
Performance: Maximum speed 157 mph (253kph)

Did You Know?

The 904's fiberglass bodies were built by the Heinkel aircraft company, but achieving consistent weight proved to be very difficult. Body thickness could be as great as 0.4-inch (10mm), and the weight difference between cars could be equivalent to carrying a passenger!

wasn't standing still, and it was clear by the beginning of 1965 that there was little development potential in the 904, particularly in the ultra-competitive arena of the European Mountainclimb championship. A spyder version was light in weight, but sacrificed the car its essential chassis stiffness. The lack of pace

was made worse in that the 904 couldn't run the new F1-size tires that were helping to give its Ferrari competition the edge.

Something else was needed—and fortunately Porsche was not slow in appreciating this.

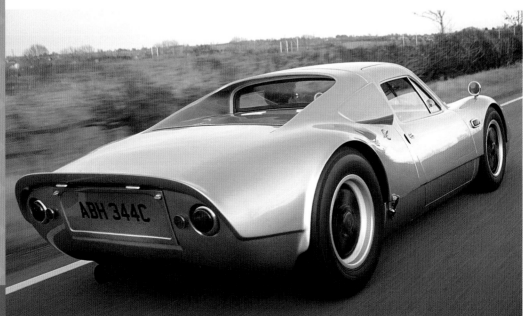

CHAPTER 3

911 BEGINNINGS

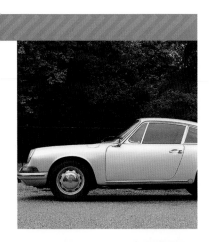

The 356 established Porsche as a serious sports car maker and put the company name in the auto press headlines worldwide. By the end of the 1950s, Ferry Porsche realized that in order for his company to take the next step, he would have to build a sports car that could establish Porsche among the big grand touring manufacturers such as Ferrari and Aston Martin. He knew a 4-cylinder sports car could never achieve that step up in caliber. Initially the engineers' thoughts focused on a new 6-cylinder engine for a development of the 356, but as the studies continued (from around 1959), it was clear a whole new car would be required.

Finding the right style, accommodation and design proved to be very difficult. Many options were considered, including stretched versions of the 356 and even full 4-seater models, but in the end, Ferry Porsche decided his company should build what they did best—a sports car.

The engine also went through several iterations. An early design for a pushrod 6-cylinder was dropped—it simply didn't reflect the cutting edge of automobile technology or produce enough power. Ferry Porsche knew that his customer enjoyed the fact that engineering developments tested on the racetracks of the world would later find their way onto the production cars. It also wasn't an option to enlarge the Carrera 4-cam 4-cylinder race engine, as it was just too complicated and noisy for a production engine.

In early 1963, Ferdinand Piëch joined Porsche as a development engineer. Piëch was the grandson of Ferdinand Porsche and nephew to Ferry. He gelled instantly with another young engineer, Hans Mezger, who had joined Porsche in 1956 and was the brains behind both the Carrera 4-cam engine's competitiveness in the late 1950s and the F1 engine's progressive improvement in 1962. If Mezger was the brilliant engineering mind at Porsche, Piëch became the catalyst for change and facilitator to turn Mezger's work into reality. Between them, the two young engineers developed an engine for the new street car in record time, an engine that would serve Porsche for decades both in production and motorsport.

To build such a revolutionary car, Porsche also had to make suitable preparations in its

engineering and manufacturing organization. The Formula One program was stopped at the end of 1962 to release both critical engineers and funds. Porsche also bought the Reutter bodyshell manufacturing facility in Zuffenhausen to give more consistent manufacturing capability. By 1963, the development entered its final stages, and by September 1963, Porsche's new sports car was revealed to the world.

The Porsche 901 made its debut at the Frankfurt Auto Show in September 1963. To anybody who had been involved in the studies for the new car just one year earlier, the result would have been amazing because it was so completely different from what was being considered earlier.

Ferdinand Alexander Porsche was responsible for the eye-catching 2+2 coupe that was unmistakably Porsche. And yet the 901 was entirely new in concept and appearance. It was F. A. Porsche's timeless profile that would ensure Porsche's business success from thereon—a sports car with an aerodynamic profile that was both elegant and utilitarian and what some called controversial. What really set the design apart were its compact torsion bar suspension and rear-engine layout—both well-proven Porsche features that delivered a roomy cabin and ample luggage space.

Just as groundbreaking was the 6-cylinder engine. The 2-liter all-aluminium, air-cooled powerplant had dry sump oiling and chain-driven overhead camshafts—revolutionary features for a production engine at the time.

Production began almost a year after Frankfurt—by which time the name had also changed to 911—and the world soon welcomed the most iconic sports car of all time.

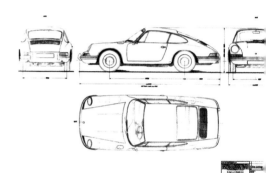

It took a while for the 911 to catch on among the wider group of drivers that Ferry Porsche needed to fuel the essential expansion of his company, but combined with a rapidly growing race reputation, the 911 soon became a must-have among knowledgeable sports car drivers. Unlike the 356, there wasn't a cabriolet version of the 911 initially, but within a few years the Targa offered semi-open driving with the added

1965 911

Engine: Air-cooled flat 6-cylinder, overhead camshaft with 2 valves per cylinder
Displacement: 1991cc
Output: 130 horsepower (95kW) at 6200 rpm
Gearbox: 5-speed manual
Chassis: Rear engine, rear wheel drive, unitary construction steel 2+2 bodyshell
Performance: Maximum speed: 130 mph; 0–62 mph in 9.1 seconds

Did You Know?

The early versions of the 911 had such tail-happy handling that by 1968 the engineers had placed nearly 90 lbs (40 kg) of weight in the front bumper to try to balance the car's weight distribution. The following year the wheelbase was extended and the weights disappeared.

protection of a stylish rollover hoop. It would be 20 years before a full 911 cabriolet model reached the marketplace.

Development initially focused on improving the handling and performance—not least because the tail-end engine location gave the car some interesting cornering habits. For 1968, an extra 2.2 inches (57mm) was added to the wheelbase, and fuel-injected models were offered. In the first phase of it development, the 6-cylinder engine went from 2 liters and 130 horsepower to 2.7 liters and 210 horsepower. *Photos courtesy Porsche AG*

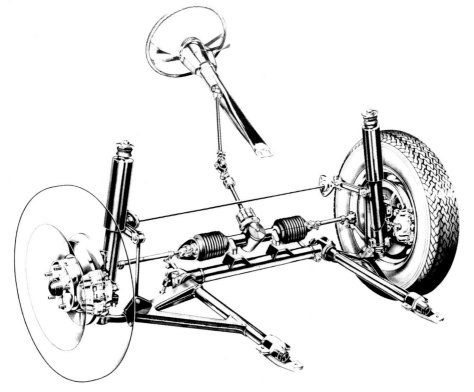

The 912 was built in the first years of 911 production when sales weren't yet established and the company's managers needed to oversee the cashflow carefully to keep the company healthy. Priced halfway between the outgoing 356SC and the 911, it offered a means to retain those existing 356 drivers who couldn't afford the financial stretch to the new model. There was also little doubt that after just 15 years of production, Porsche had its fair share of traditionalist customers. Many claimed the new

912 (1965–1968)

Engine: Air-cooled flat 4-cylinder, pushrod-operated, 2 valves per cylinder

Displacement: 1582cc

Output: 90 horsepower (66kW) at 5800rpm

Gearbox: 4-speed manual

Chassis: Rear engine, rear wheel drive, unitary construction steel 2+2 bodyshell

Performance: Maximum speed: 115mph; 0–62 mph in 13.5 seconds

911 wasn't a real Porsche because of its large size and 6-cylinder engine, so at least the 912 offered the same sound as their beloved 356s!

The 912 came with the 356SC's 1.6-liter pushrod 4-cylinder and had a less expensive interior trim, but in most other respects, this was a 911 for less money. The big feature that the 912 had over its brother was that because the 4-cylinder was lighter and less hung out behind the rear wheels, the car's general handling was more predictable. And for many,

that was a very acceptable trade-off against its lower horsepower. The less aggressive character appealed to many and the car quickly gained a

Did You Know?

The 912 was Porsche's first entry-level model and showed the company's managers that there was a profitable segment in the market for a mid-price sports car. It was a segment later filled easily by the 914, 924, 944, and Boxster.

loyal following. From its launch in spring 1965, the 912 kicked off sales of the new 911 family, and it easily outsold the 6-cylinder car every year until its replacement with the 6-cylinder 911T in 1968.

The 90-horsepower (66kW) 912 was sold alongside the regular 130-horsepower (95kW) 911, and from 1966 the top-of-the-range 160-horsepower (118kW) 911S until 1968. Today, the 912 is the investment sleeper to the 911 collector because many buyers have tended to chase down the 6-cylinder cars while ignoring the 4-cylinder versions.

Porsche had another bite at the 912 "cherry" in 1975, hoping to fill a gap between the end of production of the 914 and the introduction of the 924. Powered by a VW-based 2-liter flat-4, the car failed to perform in a difficult trading environment.

NAV 140F

In early 1963, when Ferdinand Piëch and Hans Mezger began work on the redesign of the powerplant for the car that would become the 911, they knew that the engine would have to serve Porsche both in production and in motor sport for years into the future. That's why the new engine emerged with an all-aluminium casing and such advanced features as dry sump lubrication and the forethought that would allow capacity expansions into the future. Mezger had also learned everything he needed to know about the requirements for race engine combustion chamber design from his previous projects. He also understood that while the earlier Carrera 4-cam 4-cylinder engine

911S (1968)

Engine: Air-cooled flat 6-cylinder, overhead camshaft with 2 valves per cylinder
Displacement: 1991cc
Output: 160 horsepower (95kW) at 6600rpm
Gearbox: 5-speed manual
Chassis: Rear engine, rear wheel drive, unitary construction steel 2+2 bodyshell
Performance: Maximum speed: 137mph; 0–62 mph in 7.6 seconds

produced good power, it was far too complex even for a production engine.

Consequently, parallel to the regular 901 engine, Mezger drew up a Super engine

that would be suitable for use in racing. This differed principally in using lighter, stronger materials—magnesium alloy, for instance, for some of the casings and forged connecting rods. The production Solex carbs were also replaced with more responsive Weber carburetors. The Super engine took second place to the regular engine's development, but by 1965 some race cars were running the new powerplant. It was an easy design step after good initial results to propose a new production model using much of that early Super engine experience. The 1966 911S offered 160 horsepower—up 30 horsepower on the regular car—and a whole new sporting appearance

based on its 5-spoke forged alloy wheels, sourced from Fuchs foundry.

The 911S became the top of the range model, quickly finding a niche with Porsche's more enthusiastic customers and selling in numbers that steadily increased the more Porsche won on the race tracks of the world. For the 1970 911 model year, capacity increased to 2.2 liters and

Did You Know?

The 1972 911S was the first Porsche to feature an aerodynamic device to improve the car's stability at high speed. The small lip spoiler on the front bumper was the first of many such devices to be fitted to future 911s.

by this time 911S maximum power increased to 180 horsepower (132kw), increasing again to 190 horsepower (140kW) when capacity edged up to just under 2.4 liters for 1972.

Through much of the 911's subsequent history, the leading production model has always been the "S" model.

If any single model has come to symbolize the unshakably cohesive link between motorsport and production at Porsche, it is the Carrera RS, produced as a limited edition during the 1973 model year. After 9 years of production, the 911 had become a formidable competitor in the early 1970s international grand touring and production-based sports car arena. While the prototypes captured all the headlines, it was the activities of a growing number of extremely capable private entrants (such as the Kremer brothers) that demonstrated the capabilities of the car both on race tracks and in off-road rallies. Indeed, there didn't seem to be much the 911 couldn't do when it came to any kind of motorsport. In 1967, the 911R demonstrated what could be done for a full race-prepared 911, and a few years later the 911S-T proved what a capable package the car had become as a fast, reliable customer racer. Nevertheless,

911 CARRERA RS (1973)

Engine: Air-cooled flat 6-cylinder, 2 valves per cylinder, mechanical fuel injection
Displacement: 2687cc
Output: 210 horsepower (154kW) at 6300rpm
Gearbox: 5-speed manual
Chassis: Rear engine, rear wheel drive, unitary construction steel 2+2 bodyshell
Performance: Maximum speed: 152 mph; 0–62 mph in 5.8 seconds

motorsport never stands still, and by 1971, it was clear that the limited modifications permitted by the production-based regulations were holding back the 911's competitiveness.

A new, special model was devised that used a 2.7-liter engine and a lightweight bodyshell, and to qualify the car for production series racing, Porsche had to build 500 examples. The bodyshell featured thinner sheet metal and

window glass, elimination of all the regular car's unnecessary internal trim, but the feature that became the RS's signature was the small aerodynamic spoiler on the engine cover. Quickly named the "ducktail," it underlined the performance focus that the RS offered.

There was some concern in Porsche as to whether they could sell so many cars that were so deliberately stripped out. To offset that concern, two models were offered in the showrooms—a very basic, but lightweight, version called the Sport, and a comfort version trimmed to the same standard as the 1973 911S. Porsche need not have worried—demand was very strong and by the end of the 1973 model year, no fewer than 1530 RS models had been sold. The race version, the RSR, immediately dominated.

Today, the RS is a Porsche icon, valued as much for being automotive art in its finest form as being the ultimate driving machine.

Did You Know?

In virtually its first race, the Carrera RS won its class in the Daytona 24 Hours at the beginning of 1973. The Brumos RSR driven by Hurley Haywood and Peter Gregg beat all the prototypes.

CHAPTER 4
DOING THE
UNEXPECTED

After 10 straight years of mainly performance-based development, the 911's party nearly came to an end in 1974 with the first major oil crisis to hit the developed world. When the mainly Arab-based OPEC oil producers placed an embargo on exports of gasoline and other oil-based products, the world's automotive industry went into freefall. Almost overnight, sales of "gas guzzlers" and sports cars in particular fell significantly as public attitudes to the automobile changed. It couldn't have come at a more difficult time for Porsche, which in 1972 had experienced a major Board of Management change and indecision over whether, after 10 years of production, the 911 was an obsolete product. The new boss of Porsche was Dr. Ernst Fuhrmann, the same Fuhrmann who had designed the successful 4-cam racing engine in the 1950s. From his appointment in 1972, Fuhrmann refocused Porsche's product development to give it wider appeal beyond the enthusiast drivers that made up most of Porsche's customer base. Fuhrmann wanted the 911 to be a "world" car: more refined, with less of a razor's edge, and most importantly, leading the motorsport profile of the business. His profound direction of the production car business saw Porsche through its first really difficult trading era. At the same time he laid the foundations for the 911's incredible longevity. During the 1970s, the 911 Turbo and the later 911SC established Porsche's reputation as cars that appeared to be hewn from stone, such was their perceived reliability and quality. Fuhrmann stepped down in 1981, to be replaced by the American Peter Schutz. Schutz knew a good thing when he saw it and again re-invested in the development of the 911, paving the way for first the Carrera 3.2 in late 1983 and the envelope-pushing, multi-role 959. By the 1980s, economies of the developed world were booming once more, and Porsche had the right products at the right time for more customers than it had ever experienced.

The 914 has received a mixed reception from Porsche fans. It was a great car for competition, but its boxy styling and close Volkswagen connection didn't win over everybody. But back at its launch in 1969, this joint venture between Porsche and VW drew acclaim for its clever, mid-engine design.

Placing the engine ahead of the rear axle had become the standard layout for any race car by the late 1960s, and various studies by both partners in the project suggested a mid-engine, mid-price sports car could win big sales.

The key performance factor was the car's overall weight distribution and the VW-Porsche 914 placed some 53 percent of its weight on the rear wheels, compared to the 1969 911's tail-heavy 57 percent. At 2.45 meters (96.5 inches), the 914's wheelbase was also significantly longer than even the 1969 model 911s (2.268 meters or 89.3 inches). On the 914, the extra space allowed the driver's feet to be out of the way of

914

Engine: Air-cooled flat 4-cylinder, pushrod operated 2 valves per cylinder
Displacement: 1,971cc
Output: 100 horsepower (74kW) at 5000rpm
Gearbox: 5-speed manual
Chassis: Mid-engine, rear wheel drive, unitary construction steel 2-seat bodyshell
Performance: Maximum speed: 110mph; 0–62mph in 13 seconds

the front suspension and allowed extra luggage room in front.

Two engines were available—a VW based, carbureted, air-cooled flat-4 with 80 horsepower (59kW), or the 110 horsepower flat-6 from the contemporary 911T. Impressive bodyshell packaging allowed a second luggage bay over the top of the Porsche 5-speed gearbox.

Did You Know?

The 914 underlined to Porsche the profit of having a mid-price or "entry level" sports car in the range. In six years of production, nearly 119,000 cars were delivered, significantly more than any other Porsche model at the time.

The 914 was an instant success, suggesting that those who criticized its looks were in the minority. The cabin was roomy, the pop-up headlamps fashionable, and the removable Targa roof perfect for fair weather climates. Surprisingly, the 914-6 was dropped from 1972, not least because its price was too close to the contemporary 2.4 911T. But the 4-cylinder car was steadily improved and the 1.7-liter engine was enlarged to 2 liters and 100 horsepower. This gave the 914 a sub-10 second zero to 60mph acceleration time and, combined with its long wheelbase and balanced handling, made the car a serious proposition in club motorsport. The 914 stayed in production until 1975 when VW cutbacks and the takeover of the 924 project by Porsche brought on its end.

A concept car for a turbocharged 911 was unveiled at the Paris auto show in 1973, and interest from customers was strong. By this time, Porsche was well on the way to being acknowledged as the world leader in the development of turbocharging for road racing gasoline engines. In just two years (1972 and 1973), the spectacular 917 race cars, driven by George Follmer and Mark Donohue, had come to dominate the Canadian-American (Can-Am) Challenge in North America. Unfortunately, because of the all-conquering race performance, the 917 turbos were banned at the end of that year, but in the meantime Porsche had also begun to study a blown 911 racer. And to qualify such a car in the production-based international classes, they would have to build a limited edition run of street cars.

911 TURBO 1978

Engine: Air-cooled flat 6-cylinder, single exhaust–driven turbocharger
Displacement: 3299 cc
Output: 300 horsepower at 5500rpm (European)
Gearbox: 4-speed manual
Chassis: Rear engine, rear wheel drive, unitary construction steel 2+2 bodyshell
Performance: Maximum speed: 161mph; 0–62 mph in 5.4 seconds

It took some time to get the street model right, and unlike the earlier Carrera RS limited edition, the new turbocharged car was offered as a fully equipped grand tourer. Porsche took a big gamble on producing such a car right in the middle of the world's first major oil shortage. Nevertheless,

the orders flooded in, and when the 911 Turbo was launched in 1975, plans for a limited edition of just 500 were scrapped and the model moved into mainstream production.

The first Turbos were relatively underpowered and underbraked. With 245 horsepower (260 horsepower in Europe), and using the same brakes as the earlier normally aspirated cars, the new model was faster certainly than any other street car Porsche had produced, but when pushed the new car revealed its relatively hurried development. By 1978, more development time had increased power to 265 horsepower (300 horsepower in

Did You Know?

The exhaust turbine/impeller of the 911 Turbo's turbocharger spins at between 80,000 and 100,000 rpm when the throttle is wide open.

Europe), with stronger suspension and brakes derived from the 917 sports cars.

As can be gauged by the power difference between the European and U.S. versions, the Turbo always struggled against the increasing Federal emissions regulations. From 1980 to 1986, the United States had no Turbo at all, but new improved ignition and fuel injection established

the model again from 1986. The Turbo became accepted as Porsche's flagship model. There has always been a 911 Turbo model in each of the subsequent chapters of the 911's development. The 964-bodied model (1990–1993) was the last of the single turbo cars, but with coil spring suspension, while the 993-bodied Turbo adopted two smaller turbos and the superb multi-link rear suspension.

The 1970s were an uncertain time for anybody involved in the sports car industry. The impact of the first world oil shortage in 1974–1975 changed public attitudes toward the automobile, particularly any automobile that was seen as wasteful or unnecessary. At Porsche, future direction was uncertain, but the surge of interest in the new 911 Turbo—as extravagant a sports car as any ever before—suggested that there could be hope for the future. Some in Porsche were convinced that the 911 had had its best years and the new 928 and 924 front-engined, water-cooled models pointed to a new beginning. Development of the regular

911 CARRERA 3.2

Engine: Air-cooled flat 6-cylinder, Digital Motor Electronics

Displacement: 3164cc

Output: 231 horsepower (USA: 207 horsepower) at 5900rpm

Gearbox: 5-speed manual

Chassis: Rear engine, rear wheel drive, unitary construction steel 2+2 bodyshell

Performance: Maximum speed: 152 mph; 0–62 mph in 6.1 seconds

911 slowed, although it did receive the stronger 3-liter core engine from the Turbo, but by 1980, development effort was firmly focused on the new models. The problem was the customers were not convinced the 911 was dead. As sales faltered, new Chief Executive Peter Schutz identified that Porsche couldn't afford to not push the 911. Porsche's new American boss started a comprehensive makeover. The Carrera 3.2 was launched for the start of the 1984 model year, in September 1983.

The 911's insatiable capacity for development continued, with capacity up to 3164cc (3.2 liters) thanks to using the 3.3 Turbo's

Did You Know?

The camshaft chain tensioners had always been a weak link in the already impressive reliability of Porsche air-cooled flat-6. On the Carrera 3.2, a completely new design was introduced that used the engine's oil to maintain hydraulic pressure behind the tensioner. These tensioners put an end to the worry of unexpected failure.

longer throw crankshaft. For the first time, sparking came from Bosch's Digital Motor Electronics, but ever stricter exhaust emission regulations in the United States cut maximum power from the European model's healthy 231 horsepower to 207 horsepower (although this was still better than the previous 911SC model's 180 horsepower).

Development of new versions of the basic 911 came rapidly during the Carrera 3.2 era. The Cabriolet had been previewed in 1983 and became hugely popular as a mainstream 3.2 model. Alongside this, Porsche began to offer special Turbo bodyshell models to order, which were soon adopted as mainstream catalog choices. A move to the more user-friendly G50 gearbox and a larger clutch for the 1987 model year transformed the Carrera's appeal. The years 1984–1989 were marked by two other notable limited editions in the form of the Carrera Club Sport and the Speedster (red finish, below). The Club Sport was a lightweight special that used a slightly reworked engine to deliver an impressive 0 to 60 mph of just 5.2 seconds. The Speedster used a raked screen and molded plastic rear cover to recall the style of the classic 1950s model.

The mid-1980s were something of a golden period for Porsche. Not only had the 911 been completely revised and updated with the new Carrera 3.2 model, but in racing, McLarens were dominating with the Porsche-designed TAG-turbo engine, and the 956/962 prototypes were unbeatable in endurance racing. It was hardly surprising that the rally fans within Porsche wanted to get in on the act. Porsche had shown the "Gruppe B" design concept for an all-wheel

959

Engine: Air-cooled flat 6-cylinder (with water-cooled cylinder heads), twin turbos and intercoolers
Displacement: 2849cc
Output: 450 horsepower (330kW) at 6500rpm
Gearbox: 6-speed manual, 4-wheel drive
Chassis: Unitary construction steel 2+2 bodyshell with aluminium hood, doors, PU bumpers
Performance: Maximum speed: 196 mph; 0–62 mph in 3.9 seconds

drive rally car in 1983. The rally regulations required 200 examples to be built, and such was the interest from potential street car customers that development continued. A prototype all-wheel drive 911 won the 12,000 km Paris-Dakar "desert" rally in 1984, but it took some time to develop and refine the product to the point that customer cars could be sold. By this time, Porsche had decided the car would be a showcase of its development capabilities and, to

Did You Know?

Porsche significantly undersold the 959, and at the time lightly used cars were being offered speculatively at some four times the ex-factory price. Prices today remain significantly ahead of the original selling price as they become sought-after examples of an engineer-dominated Porsche that has long since disappeared.

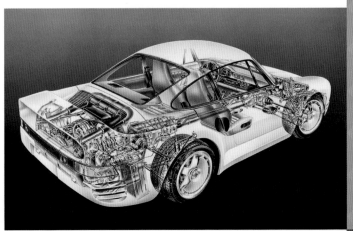

demonstrate its versatility, produced versions that were capable of competing in the most extreme off-road rallies and also racing at places like Le Mans. All the time a third development path worked on producing a luxury express for street use. It was a massive commitment and such was the level of advanced technology applied, customer cars did not begin deliveries until 1987. In the end, 283 cars were built through 1987–88. Despite the long wait, drivers were not disappointed. With its 450 horsepower (330kW) twin turbo engine, 6-speed gearbox, and all-wheel drive, the 959 proved to be a very confident performer. While perhaps looking a little dated today, at the time the looks were considered sensational. The car owed little to the regular Carrera 3.2, and each car was essentially a hand-built prototype of the highest quality.

The 959 is an important stepping stone in the 911 story as it previewed all-wheel drive and water cooling on the street 911 and gave glimpses of where styling thinking was headed in the future. *Photos courtesy Porsche AG*

CHAPTER 5
THE GOLDEN ERA

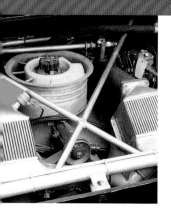

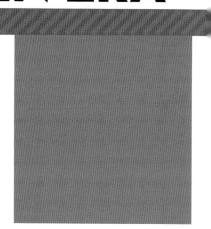

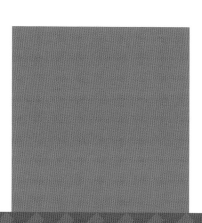

Ferdinand Piëch was the grandson of Professor Ferdinand Porsche. Piëch grew up steeped in the values and ambition that surrounded the Porsche family and its recovery from the ruins of the Second World War. After completing his engineering education at a prestigious Swiss university, Piëch joined Porsche in 1963 in the Experimental department and immediately began to rip through the company like a whirlwind.

These were turbulent times within Porsche. The 356 had established the business as a leading sports car manufacturer, and the 550s and RSKs had carved an illustrious reputation for the company on the racetracks of the world. Porsche was one of the stars of Germany's *Wirtschaftswunder* ("economic miracle")—the spectacular regeneration of that country's economy out of the ruins of World War II. But the pioneers who had built Porsche with their blood, sweat, and tears in the late 1940s and 1950s were perhaps looking too conservative in a climate of explosive innovation that the 1960s appeared to require of any ambitious company. Ferry Porsche was not slow to appreciate the importance of keeping his company innovating and expanding. He had stopped the 1962 F1 effort to release resources for the upcoming development and production of the new sports car (the 911). In motorsport, the cancellation of the F1 program left the company with something of an identity crisis. In endurance racing, technology was changing fast, and while the new 904 proved itself as a class winner at Le Mans in 1964, it was quickly shown to be behind the pace for 1965.

The young Ferdinand Piëch immediately set about ensuring that Porsche's motorsport future was secure, but he also had a vision to take Porsche to the very top of the sports car racing tree. He wanted Porsche to win the big races overall, not just compete for the class victories. With guidance from Ferry Porsche, Piëch brought a revolutionary zeal to engineering at Porsche, ruffling the feathers of many of the older engineers, but bringing an absolutely focused energy and leadership to the activity. Importantly, he also found a soul-mate in the brilliant mind of Hans Mezger, another relatively young graduate engineer with a finely tuned mathematical and engineering brain. Their first target after Piëch joined Porsche in 1963 was to ensure the new 911 model would be suitable for both street production and racing. While keenly aware that racing should only be used to improve the quality and prestige of the street cars, Piëch also set about developing a dedicated race development team that would be capable—in the future—of winning Le Mans for Porsche.

By 1965, he was appointed head of the Experimental department. That season, it became clear that the factory's principal race car, the 904, was increasingly uncompetitive against new models that took advantage of the latest F1 tire technology. Nowhere was this disadvantage more clear than on the mountain courses of the European Hillclimb Championship. Winning 6 of the 7 previous championships, this had almost become Porsche's property. But in 1965, Ferrari introduced their beautiful 206 Dino, using the small 15-inch wheels and tires from the current F1 cars. The red car proved to be effortlessly faster than the 904, even when Piëch's men replaced the heavy (but strong) fiberglass coupe body with a lightweight spyder body. By early August of that year, Piëch tasked Mezger to build a brand-new tubular spaceframe prototype to try and beat the Dino on the hills. In a spectacular display of motivation, skill, and confidence,

Mezger led a team that worked 24/7, designing and building a brand-new car in record time. That car competed in its first race, at Ollon-Villars in Switzerland, just 24 days after they had the approval to do it! The new car didn't win there, but driver Gerhard Mitter was some 30 seconds quicker than in the old 904 spyder. It did win the next event.

Meanwhile, there was an urgent need to provide a new production race car for customers to use in the 1966 season. The 906 proved to be a very effective halfway house in the transition of Porsche's race engineering between the sheet steel framed 904 and the Ollon-Villars-derived 910. The nimble 910 was soon superceded for long-distance endurance racing by a new car, the 907. Still using the F1-derived 8-cylinder engine, it was the first Porsche to be available in long- and short-tail variants (depending on whether the circuit was fast or twisty, respectively). When

Hans Mezger improved the engine to 2.2 liters and designed in greater reliability, 907s finished 1–2–3 in the 1968 Daytona 24 Hours. After this victory, there followed in quick succession the 908 (which finally won for Porsche the manufacturers' World Championship) and the remarkable 917. Each one of these prototype sports cars is memorable, but as a group, they represent an unsurpassed family of race cars.

The spectacular Ollon-Villars development had triggered a period of high-intensity progress at Porsche that could probably never be repeated. By Hans Mezger's own words, in the 1960s, 10 new road and race cars and 5 new engines were developed and built by what would be considered an incredibly small team by today's standards. The cars and engines they produced in the short period from 1965 to 1973 represent the very best of Porsche and are at the foundation of the company's rich heritage today.

The 908 was the first car to win the World Manufacturers' Championship for Porsche. Derived from the earlier 907 and with a brand-new 3-liter engine, the new car debuted at the Nürburgring 1000km in May 1968. This came after a whirlwind development of both chassis and engine.

The regulations had changed for 1968, outlawing the big capacity sports cars of the previous years, such as the Ford Mk IVs, Ferrari 330P4s, and the high-winged Chaparral. Porsche believed there was a real chance that a 3-liter prototype would have the capability to beat the ageing 5-liter Ford GT40s that were still permitted to race (as limited edition production sports cars).

By 1967, Porsche's Hans Mezger was testing an experimental 4-camshaft 6-cylinder engine not only as a race development but also as a possible next step for the street 911. When the 3-liter car was approved, it was a straightforward process to add two more cylinders to make an 8-cylinder 3-liter. By this time Ferdinand Piëch had decreed that every prototype starting a world championship endurance race should have a new chassis. This was a psychological (and expensive) tactic to give the factory drivers more confidence in their cars at a time when there were serious safety concerns about the consequences of a broken chassis.

1971 908/3

Engine: Air-cooled flat 8-cylinder, 4 chain-driven camshafts
Displacement: 2997cc
Output: 360 horsepower (265kW) at 8400rpm
Gearbox: 5-speed manual
Performance: Not available

It took most of 1968 to ease out the bugs from the new car (including designing out a severe engine vibration), but for 1969, the team found the reliability they needed. A new spyder version (the 908/2) was a big favorite with the drivers. Unfortunately, the 908 still proved unable to win the big prize for Porsche in 1968 or 1969.

Did You Know?

The 1970–71 908/3s carried "ace" playing card symbols as a tribute to the Ferdinand Porsche–designed and similarly "suited" Austro-Daimler Sascha sports cars that won the Targa Florio in 1922.

At Le Mans, the factory cars were defeated both years by the robust GT40s entered by the John Wyer Automotive Engineering team. The defeat would simply spur the men at Porsche on to greater efforts.

The 908/3 emerged from the industrious Porsche workshops in 1970. Completely redesigned with the gearbox ahead of the rear axle line (to improve its turn-in agility), the 908/3 was raced by the factory at the twisty Targa Florio and Nürburgring courses in 1970 and 1971. The nimble 908/3 was a driver favorite and saw extended service in private hands (and with turbo engines) well into the mid-1970s.
Historical photos courtesy Porsche AG

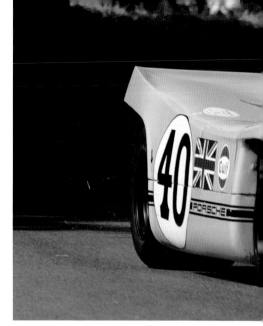

The Porsche 917 is arguably the greatest racing car ever made. This was a racing sports car built to win one race—France's 24 Hours of Le Mans. Porsche had entered the famous race almost since they began assembling cars in Stuttgart—with the first entry being made in 1951—but despite several near misses, they couldn't capture an elusive first overall win.

In 1965, Professor Ferdinand Porsche's 28-year-old nephew Ferdinand Piëch became technical director at Porsche. Like his grandfather, Piëch was possessed of the rare talents of being able to see an end goal

917K

Engine: 180-degree (flat), air-cooled 12-cylinder, All-aluminium with 2 valves per cylinder and mechanical fuel injection

Displacement: Initially 4494cc (1969) rising to 4999cc (1971)

Output: Initially 585 horsepower (1969) rising to 630 horsepower (1971)

Gearbox: 4- or 5-speed with reverse. All forward gears with reverse

Brakes: Internally ventilated steel disc brakes all around with 4-piston alloy calipers

Performance: Maximum speed approximately 246 mph at Le Mans

and a wide-ranging ability to drive his vision to completion. And Piëch wanted Le Mans for Porsche. His good fortune was to have a brilliant young engineer/mathematician called Hans Mezger working for him, as well as some of the most experienced race development engineers in the world.

The 917 first turned a wheel in early 1969 and was notable because Porsche had to build 25 examples of what was a cutting-edge racer before they were permitted to enter the car. The 917 was the fastest race car Porsche had ever made, and at first it was terrifying to drive.

It was nearly uncontrollable above 180 mph. But by 1970, and with a fortuitous link-up with the ace British John Wyer team, the 917 was winning races and breaking records wherever it appeared.

Did You Know?

The 917's race winning average speed for the 1971 Spa 1000 km was 154.77 mph, which stands as an all-time record for the fastest road race in history.

At the old 8.76-mile Spa road race track, the 917s were lapping faster than the contemporary grand prix cars. At Le Mans, Piëch's dream was achieved in 1970 and 1971, and for the extensive Mulsanne straight, Porsche developed a special long-tail body that gave the cars a maximum speed of some 246 mph.

The 917 was banned from endurance racing at the end of 1971, but meanwhile Porsche had turned its attention to the North American CanAm Challenge. A new chapter for the 917 was about to begin. *Historical photos courtesy Porsche AG*

The CanAm Challenge Cup was tailor-made for Porsche. When the FIA decided to ban the 5-liter cars altogether from endurance racing at the end of 1971, Porsche quit that scene and readily turned its attention to CanAm. Like hillclimbing, CanAm was another virtually unlimited formula. The North American series, which combined every motor racing superlative required to ensure success (having an outlaw

1973 917/30

Engine: Air-cooled flat 12-cylinder, twin-turbo
Displacement: 5374cc
Output: 1100 horsepower (806kW) at 8000rpm
Gearbox: 4-speed manual
Chassis: 2-seat spyder, multi-tubular aluminium spaceframe
Performance: Maximum speed approximately 207 mph

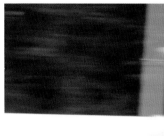

philosophy on speed, noise, spectacle, and cash), had been dominated since its beginnings by large-capacity Detroit V-8s. The big winners through the late 1960s proved to be McLaren, led by Bruce McLaren himself. Porsche's factory driver Jo Siffert raced a 917 spyder (called the 917PA, after the main sponsor Porsche-Audi) in 1969 and again in 1970. So tempted were the Porsche people by CanAm even then that

Did You Know?

In 1975, Mark Donohue and a specially prepared 917/30 set a new world closed course speed record at the Talladega Raceway in Alabama, with a best average speed of 221.120 mph (355.78 kph) over one flying lap.

Hans Mezger built and tested a 16-cylinder engine as a possible answer to the Detroit V-8s. That monster engine never raced, because by then Mezger saw the potential of successfully turbocharging a road race engine. Through 1971, Mezger's small development team worked to refine this raw turbo power. And when, at the end of that year, Porsche teamed up with experienced race entrant American Roger Penske and his engineer/driver Mark Donohue, the winning formula for a turbocharged CanAm car quickly came together.

The 917/10 was Porsche's first turbo car, and while Donohue did most of the development in early 1972, he suffered a crash in testing and it was his teammate George Follmer who took the title. The domination continued in 1973, and this time Donohue did win the title he deserved. By this time, the twin turbo flat-12 engine was producing a comfortable 1100 horsepower wide open.

The dominance was too much for CanAm's organizers and the other teams and at the end of 1973, regulations were introduced that effectively ruled out the turbo Porsches. Porsche quit. The 917/30 gave Porsche a legacy of technology that kept it at the front of world motorsport for the next 25 years and provided the flagship 911 Turbo for its production model lineup. *Historical photos courtesy Porsche AG*

In 1974, in a test program for new GT-based categories, Porsche raced a lightweight RSR powered by a 500 horsepower, 2.14-liter turbocharged engine—calling it the RSR-turbo. The installation was derived directly from the CanAm 917/30, using a single turbo to compress the inlet air to all 6 cylinders. It was an animal to drive, but second places at both the Le Mans and the Watkins Glen proved that Porsche had found real race turbo engine reliability. Unfortunately, the rulemakers further restricted the rules to make the cars

1978 935/78

Engine: 6-cylinder with water-cooled cylinder heads and air-cooled cylinders, 4 valves per cylinder, twin turbo

Displacement: 3211cc

Output: 750 horsepower (550kW) at 8200rpm

Gearbox: 4-speed manual

Chassis: Pressed steel central cabin with front/rear aluminium subframe and roll-over cage

Performance: Maximum speed approximately 223 mph

more production-based. The eventual classes run in a revived World Championship of Makes from 1976 were for lightly modified production cars (Group 4) and fully modified production cars (Group 5). There was also a class (Group 6) for full prototypes. For Group 4, Porsche produced the 934, developed from the street 911 Turbo for private entrants. For Group 5, there was the 590 horsepower 935—for the factory entries and professional race teams.

The 935 proved to be a very effective weapon and the factory team won that year's championship. A modified version was developed for 1977 featuring considerably improved aerodynamics and twin turbos for the engine, which now delivered a maximum of 630

Did You Know?

Nowhere was the 935's success more obvious than in the IMSA Camel GT series in North America. In one race, the 1981 Daytona 24 Hours, no fewer than 15 935s were entered and 9 of the first 10 qualifiers were 935s.

horsepower. The championship was won again, but not least because of the competitiveness of several of the factory's racing customers, such as the Kremer brothers and Georg Loos. In the coming years, the factory focused on improving power and reliability for its customers. Two

special models stand out, however. In 1977, Zuffenhausen produced a one-off 1.4-liter turbo engine for a lightweight 935 they called "Baby." The 935 Baby raced in just two national championship races, winning one. The other special was the remarkable 935/78, which can

really only be described as a fully modified car with a brand-new engine featuring water-cooled cylinder heads. This car was nicknamed "Moby Dick" and was capable of 220 mph (below).

It fell to a private team to win Le Mans with a 935. The heavily modified Kremer brothers 935K3 model became the equipment of choice for professional race teams in sports car racing until the introduction of the ground effect prototypes in the early 1980s. *Historical photos courtesy Porsche AG*

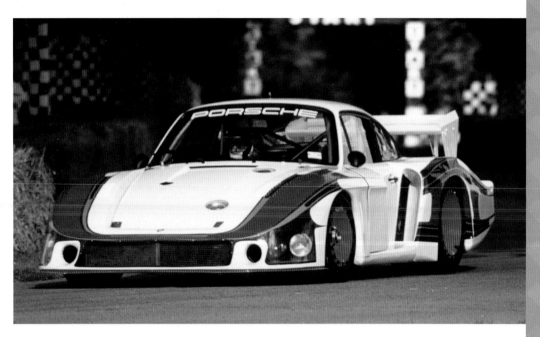

The 936 remains one of the most successful race cars ever to emerge from Porsche. The decision to build a Group 6 car was made in the fall of 1975 and was notable for the minimal budget used in its development. The aluminium tubular spaceframe chassis was derived from the CanAm 917/10, and the 2.14-liter engine descended directly from the 1974 RSR-turbo. The 5-speed gearbox came from the 917/30.

The 936's first race was at Monza, where new driver pairing Jacky Ickx and Jochen Mass cruised to victory. Partnered by Gijs van Lennep, Ickx also took a 936 to victory at Le Mans despite a long stop for a broken exhaust. The following year Ickx helped the team to victory again, but only after an inspired piece of night driving. The engine also expired 45 minutes from the end and only finished after Jürgen Barth drove a very careful two laps on 5 cylinders to take the checkered flag.

A high-budget Renault team finally beat Porsche at the French course in 1978, despite Porsche having a new 4-valve engine with water-cooled cylinder heads for the 2 of the 3 936s entered.

In 1979, the entries came far too late after a last-minute sponsorship deal and both factory cars ran into problems with a best result of only third. By senior management decree, there were to be no factory 936s entered in 1980 (while the race team focused on the 924 Carrera GTs), but the private entrant Reinhold Joest and Jacky Ickx raced a car that looked very much like a 936 to second place.

1981 936/81

Engine: 6-cylinder, 4 valves per cylinder water/air cooled with gear-driven overhead camshafts
Displacement: 2650cc
Output: 620 horsepower (455kW) at 8000rpm
Gearbox: 4-speed manual
Chassis: 2-seat spyder, multi-tubular aluminium spaceframe
Performance: Maximum speed approximately 230 mph

In 1981, two 936s were taken out of the Porsche museum and given a thorough development makeover. They were fitted with the 2.65-liter turbo from the cancelled Indycar program (and converted to run on gasoline). Jacky Ickx/Derek Bell cruised to victory. That made a total of three Le Mans wins for the car that had been created almost as an afterthought.

Did You Know?

In its early testing and races, the 936 was painted flat black. The color choice had started almost as a joke, when Porsche didn't want Renault to discover its prototype plans. Nevertheless, main sponsor Martini asked for the base color to be changed back to the more traditional white.

CHAPTER 6
WATER-COOLED CRUSADERS

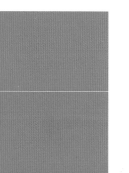

The 1970s were a period of significant change for Porsche, influenced by events inside and outside the business. World economic conditions went through convulsions in the wake of the 1973–1974 Middle East oil embargo and the auto industry as a whole looked severely threatened. Nobody really doubted that economies would recover in time, but by 1975 public attitudes to the automobile had fundamentally shifted.

By the end of 1972, Porsche's management had also changed. Ferry Porsche had decided that his business was bigger than his family. He wasn't satisfied with a likely management succession path that included all the highly competitive members of his and the Piëch families. Through 1971–1972, Ferry and the other family members working for Porsche stepped back from the day-to-day running of the business, retaining their interest through a holding company. Replacing Ferry at the top of a new, public stock company Porsche AG was Dr. Ernst Fuhrmann—the same Fuhrmann who had been responsible for the 4-cam "Carrera" engine.

Unfortunately, Fuhrmann's first tasks included having to completely restructure Porsche's product plan in the light of a cancelled VW project to replace the Beetle. The engineers at Porsche's Weissach development center were well advanced on this project when it was cancelled in late 1971. To busy the engineers, they were put to work refreshing the 911 (which would emerge for the 1974 models) and designing a brand-new V-8-engined grand tourer. By this time the 911 was considered only to have a few more years of useful life left and the new model would be its replacement.

Project 928 was designed through the worst of the world economic crisis of the mid-1970s. The design brief ensured that it would be able to meet a moving target of changing attitudes to vehicle safety, emissions, and noise, while at the same time showcasing Porsche's expertise as sports car makers. That climate of change explains the 928's almost conventional layout of front-engine, rear-wheel drive. And when it did appear in 1977, its freshness pointed to a whole new era for Porsche.

Another cancelled VW project led to the adoption of the 924. In 1971, VW was enthusiastic for a new sports car launched on the back of the mid-engine 914's success. But the 2-seat 914 required a good driver to handle it well. To make the new car more appealing in the general sports car marketplace, VW wanted an easy-to-handle and practical 2+2 package—and like the 928, project EA425 evolved as a front-engine, rear-wheel-drive sports car. However, the 1974 oil crisis reversed VW's attitudes to sports cars.

With eight prototypes running and over $50 million spent, EA425 was cancelled.

Porsche, however, remained bullish about the prospects for the sports car and bought up the project. The sales of the 914 had not gone unnoticed by all involved in the Porsche supply chain, and dealers wanted another lower cost sports car to sell alongside the 911. By the end of 1975, EA425 had been given a Porsche identity, and with production sub-contracted to the VW plant in Neckarsulm, the 924 was born.

Over the coming years, Porsche held on to what became a roller coaster ride in this segment of the marketplace. Continuous development brought on the 924 Turbo, then the 944 in late 1981 (with an all-new Porsche engine). The 944 was a huge success in the mid-1980s, but ran out of breath by 1990. Its replacement, the 968, was just too little too late to take on the increasingly strong Pacific Rim competition. But Porsche has never forgotten the revenue potential of its smaller sports car models.

The 928 was always going to be priced at or above the top-of-the-range 911. Even during the 1974 oil crisis, Porsche held on to the belief that this model had to be a grand touring sports car. The project leader was Helmut Flegl, fresh out of developing the CanAm 917/30, and it is no surprise the 928 bristles with motorsport experience. The 2+2 passenger layout did indeed point toward the mainstream, with a front engine driving the rear wheels. The engine was all-new, a 4.5-liter alloy V-8—smooth, powerful, with 240 horsepower, and relatively quiet compared to the air-cooled 911. The rear-mounted transmission gave the car more balance and could be either manual or automatic. Thanks to this and a rear multi-link, coil spring suspension design, the handling was also in a different league.

The 928 launched in late 1977 to almost universal praise, but it wasn't a 911. It was good—very good—and many loved the fact that it didn't have the 911's edgy personality. Inevitably there was a cry for more power, and by 1979 the 928S offered 300 horsepower from a 4.7-liter engine. Nevertheless, sales remained stubbornly unimpressive as the world's economies endured another cyclical slump at the start of the 1980s. Worse for the 928 was the fact that 911 sales were holding up. The chances of Porsche discontinuing the 911 were remote, particularly as the 928S failed to meet North American and Japanese emissions regulations and, as a result, was not sold there.

It was only after brand-new 4-valve cylinder heads and digital motor electronics were incorporated into the engine design that the

1992 928GTS

Engine: Liquid-cooled V-8-cylinder, double overhead camshafts, 4 valves per cylinder
Displacement: 5397cc
Output: 350 horsepower at 5700rpm
Gearbox: 5-speed manual or 4-speed automatic
Chassis: Front engine, rear wheel drive unitary construction steel bodyshell with 2+2 cabin
Performance: Maximum speed: 171 mph; 0–62mph: 5.9 seconds (auto)

new 928S4 found its way back into these markets. The new model was available from late 1985 and in Europe from the following year (still as the S4 to a new facelifted and worldwide specification).

By the 1990s, the original 1970s styling was beginning to look a little dated, but with detail appearance changes, the 5.4-liter, 350 horsepower 928GTS tried to evoke a new freshness. But facing continued falling sales and an internal need at Porsche to prepare for the new Boxster and 911 generation, the 928 was discontinued in 1995.

Did You Know?

The 928 has always had a reputation as a cruiser. Its market segment was defined by the fact that over 70 percent of 928S4 sales were in automatic form.

It was perhaps inevitable that there would be a 924 Turbo. With all that turbocharged expertise within Porsche, a blown version was also almost essential. From its launch back in late 1975, the 2-liter 924 had been (unfairly) branded as "not a real Porsche" by enthusiasts, who pointed to its Audi-sourced 4-cylinder engine. The heart of any Porsche is its engine, and this one had distinctly unsporting origins, being used also as a light commercial powerplant. But the 924 Turbo's engines were assembled in

1981 924 TURBO

Engine: Liquid-cooled 4-cylinder, single overhead camshaft, 2 valves per cylinder, single turbocharger

Displacement: 1984cc

Output: 177 horsepower at 5500rpm

Gearbox: 5-speed manual

Chassis: Front engine, rear wheel drive unitary construction steel bodyshell with 2+2 cabin

Performance: Maximum speed: 143 mph; 0–62 mph: 7.7 seconds

Zuffenhausen, using a new Porsche-designed cylinder head and a single turbo-mounted low down on the exhaust side of the strongly tilted engine, with a long inlet duct feeding the K-Jetronic fuel injection. If the regular 924's maximum power was a fairly lackluster 125 horsepower, then the first turbocharged model delivered—for the European markets—a much more impressive 170 horsepower. A North American version suffered from emissions restrictions and produced just 143 horsepower.

Did You Know?

The 924 Carrera GTR race car produced up to 450 horsepower, accelerated from 0 to 60 mph in just 4.3 seconds, and had a top speed of 190 mph. On the long Le Mans straights, it was still very slow compared to the 935K3s, which were capable of up to 220 mph.

The Turbo version stood out from the regular 924 by virtue of its extra vents in the front and the attractive NACA duct in the front hood. As always with faster Porsche variants, there was a host of additional improvements under the skin, including ventilated rotors and five lug attachments for the alloy wheels.

This was a time at Porsche when the water-cooled models were receiving preferential treatment in development over the 911 and in late 1980, a completely revised "Series 2" version used digital motor electronics and produced 177 horsepower (154 horsepower in the United States).

On the back of declining 924 sales, the 924 Turbo always struggled to achieve wide acceptance, but for those enthusiasts who were unable to stretch to a 911, it offered a lot of "bang for the buck." In its appeal, it was similar to the earlier 914/6. The 924 Turbo's exclusivity over the regular 924 was ensured by production numbers of some 10 percent of the unblown version.

The 924 Carrera GT limited edition was developed from the 924 Turbo and three modified cars ran at Le Mans in 1980. All three finished (in varying states of health), but in doing so, they gave the turbocharged 924s a good measure of race-proven pedigree.

The 944 is a vehicle borne of expediency more than plan. When Porsche had bought the 924 from VW, the deal included a commitment that VW would supply up to 100,000 engines. Given that 924 production began in January 1976, and the 50,000th car was delivered in April 1978, Porsche needed a strategy for when their engine supply ran out. Work began on a brand-new inline 4-cylinder in 1977 with the aim of using as much of the manufacturing technology and knowledge as possible from the development of the 928's V-8.

At this stage, the intention was simply to drop the new engine in place of the old, offering drivers a whole new performance package compared to the outgoing VW-Audi-powered version. The 100,000th 924 was delivered in February 1981, just after Porsche gained a new CEO. Peter Schutz directed that the proposed evolution 924 plans be scrapped and that the very attractive bodyshell from the limited edition 924 Carrera GT be used with the new engine.

The new 160-horsepower (150 horsepower in the United States) 2.5-liter 944 launched in September 1981 and was an immediate seller. Porsche had successfully rejuvenated its front-engine sports car offering. A 220 horsepower Turbo version followed in 1985, and this became the basis for a very successful one-model race series. The Porsche Turbo Cup was a mainly Germany-based championship, but in future years it became the springboard to the Carrera Cup and the Grand Prix–supporting Supercup. The 944 Turbo evolved into a class-leading 250 horsepower supercar in 1989 and remains arguably one of the most versatile all-around Porsche sports cars.

In 1986, a third model was added to the 944 family with the 944S. Power was increased to 190 horsepower, thanks mainly to a 4-valve cylinder head. Still with 2.5 liters, the car itself turned out to be disappointing, and it wasn't until the capacity was lifted to 3 liters with the Turbo-bodied 944S2 in 1989 that the model found the maturity it needed. Arguably, the 944S2 was the car the 944 should always have been, but evolution and development always take time.

By 1989, 4-cylinder production in Neckasulm had passed 300,000, but demonstrating how fast markets can turn around, in 1991, all 4-cylinder production returned to Zuffenhausen.

1991 944S2

Engine: Liquid-cooled 4-cylinder, double overhead camshaft, 4 valves per cylinder
Displacement: 2990cc
Output: 211 horsepower at 5800 rpm
Gearbox: 5-speed manual
Chassis: Front engine, rear wheel drive unitary construction steel bodyshell with 2+2 cabin
Performance: Maximum speed: 149 mph; 0–62mph: 6.9 seconds

Did You Know?

Apart from slightly enlarged inlet ports, the 4-valve cylinder heads on the 944S2 were derived directly from those on the 5-liter 928S4. The cylinder block used coolant and oil circulation technology first perfected on the Porsche-designed F1 TAG-turbo engine.

In 1981, Porsche had successfully reinvented the 924 as the 944, and 10 years later it believed the 968 could do the same again.

Launched in late 1991, the 968 was said to be some 83 percent new, but there was no mistaking the close relationship with the earlier model. That meant that unloved features, such as the 1970s panel gaps and the bonded rear side windows, were carried over. It didn't help that the 968 was launched into the teeth of a very severe world economic recession, but the bottom line was that the 968 bombed. Disappointing sales weren't

1992 968

Engine: Liquid-cooled inline 4-cylinder, double overhead camshafts, 4 valves per cylinder
Displacement: 2990cc
Output: 240 horsepower at 6200 rpm
Gearbox: 5-speed manual or 4-speed automatic (Tiptronic)
Chassis: Front engine, rear wheel drive unitary construction steel bodyshell with 2+2 cabin
Performance: Maximum speed: 156 mph; 0–62mph in 6.5 seconds

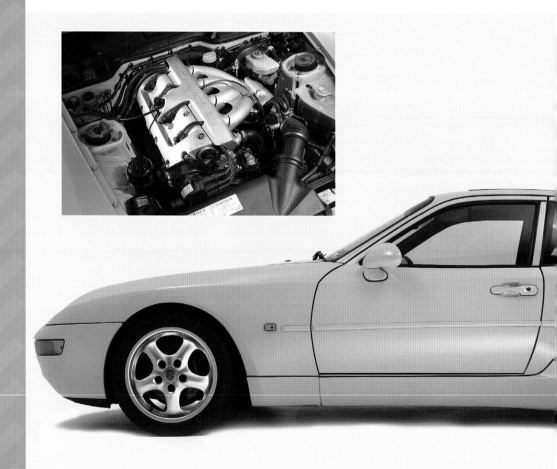

helped when it was universally slammed by the automobile press, who wondered what drivers were really getting new in a package that could trace its origins back 18 years.

The reality was that the 968 was a very good sports car indeed. Despite having only 4 cylinders, the 240-horsepower all-alloy engine featured variable valve timing for the first time in any Porsche. This helped give the 968 a power flexibility that many a 6- and 8-cylinder engine would have died for. The fuel injection was fully integrated into the digital motor electronics and the new Motronic system also used a hot-wire arrangement in the inlet ducting to far more accurately determine the fuel mixture and ignition timing. And while the technology was impressive, a 2-into-1 larger-bore exhaust gave the 968 a superb twin-cam roar on hard acceleration! The 968 came in both coupe and cabriolet forms, and with ABS-assisted brakes and perfectly

Did You Know?

When sales of the 968 didn't meet expectations, Porsche launched a stripped-out version called the 968 Club Sport. This perfectly balanced, 240-horsepower sprinter remains one of the most effective street cars for the track you can buy.

balanced handling it was, like all the 944s before it, far more sure-footed than the 911.

Porsche did toy with the idea of a turbocharged version, but while prototypes were run, a production 968 Turbo did not see any dealer's showrooms. That was probably a good thing as the Turbo versions of both the 924 and 944 were not considered commercial successes (despite their superb dynamics).

The 968 ceased production in 1995 after less than 4 years and under 13,000 cars produced, making way for the new generation of Porsches that were to arrive shortly—the Boxster and the new 911.

CHAPTER 7
RACING EXCELLENCE

The 1980s were the most successful ever in motorsport for Porsche. The success came on the back of industry-leading technology in turbocharging and the blossoming maturity of the small core of engineers that made up the racing department.

The success of the 936 in the 1970s had proven to be a revelation to Porsche and underlined their command of sports car race design. Unreliability at Le Mans in 1977 led to the development of new water-cooled cylinder heads for the twin turbo flat-six. Porsche's engine wizard Hans Mezger planned a family of race engines that would not only be suitable for endurance racing but also allow Porsche to compete at Indianapolis. Lobbying from the American sales organization resulted in a development for renowned Californian entrant (and Porsche 935 racer) Ted Field. Field's Indycar driver Danny Ongais was "Rookie of the Year" at Indianapolis in 1977, and had qualified second in 1978. The 2.65-liter single turbo ran on methanol and was notable for having no cooling fan—methanol had very good cooling properties. Unfortunately, the engine never had an opportunity to show what it could do in public. A last-minute rule change gave Porsche an excuse to cancel the project at a time when production car sales were struggling. Nevertheless, the engine was not forgotten and became the basis of Porsche's new challenger in the FIA Group C endurance racing formula due to start in 1982. A modified Indy engine, still with a capacity of 2.65 liters but running on gasoline, powered the evergreen 936 to victory at Le Mans in 1981. Porsche had decided to use the race as a test for the new Group C specification and the Indy engine proved to be perfect for this new role.

Group C was a fuel consumption formula, so each car was restricted in the amount of fuel that could be used during a race. The 956 was a brand-new race coupe—the first race Porsche to use a full aluminium chassis (rather than the older tube frame) and ground effect underbody aerodynamics. The car was immediately competitive and began a string of long-distance victories worldwide.

In 1984, a longer wheelbase version was developed—the 962—that allowed the car to race in the hugely popular IMSA race series in the United States. The 962, entered by a number of innovative and resourceful teams and using specially tuned sprint engines developed by the Californian engine tuner

Andial, dominated IMSA for the next 5 years. In 1985, the endurance racers also switched to the 962. The 956 and 962 became the definitive sports race cars of the 1980s and even when the competition began to eat away at the car's supremacy, private entrants still competed effectively with the model. During its eligibility in world sports car racing between 1982 and 1994—an incredible 12 years—cars from the 956/962 family would win Le Mans no fewer than 7 times.

Porsche's motorsport success through the 1980s also had another, very high profile, side. Since Porsche produced the remarkable "Baby" version of the 935 back in 1977, Formula One entrants had been beating a path to Porsche's

door. The Baby used a 1.4-liter turbo, which placed it very near being eligible for the current Formula One regulations for a turbo engine. But the Porsche people, particularly engine wizard Hans Mezger, knew that the air-cooled flat six wasn't suitable for F1. Nevertheless, alongside ever-improving versions of the air-cooled engine, Mezger kept a close watch on what was happening in F1.

When top F1 team McLaren made an approach to Porsche in 1981, a deal was quickly done that resulted in what Ferdinand Piëch has called Porsche's "motor of the 1980s.'" The TAG turbo (named after the principal sponsor of the project) was a state-of-the-art V-6 twin turbo with 1.5 liters capacity. The Porsche-McLaren relationship was extremely productive. The new engine debuted in mid-1983, and drivers Niki Lauda and Alain Prost won three consecutive world championships with the Porsche-designed engine. Nevertheless, Porsche's most senior management wanted to switch the company's attention to the U.S. market and the F1 focus was lost from around 1986. A new Indianapolis car, powered by a brand-new engine and using much of the technology from the TAG V-6 development, began testing in 1987. That development was progressing well, with the first win coming in 1989, before the project was brought to an untimely halt by the same factors that had stalled further development of a new endurance racer.

The Porsche 956/962 family of prototypes were the definitive race sports cars of the 1980s. From its introduction in early 1982, the first version—the 956—largely dominated FIA endurance racing around the world. Not only was the car technically very competitive, using an engine directly developed from the still-born Indycar project of 1980, but the works cars were driven by some of the best long-distance racers of the day. Jacky Ickx, Derek Bell, Jochen Mass, Stefan Bellof, Hurley Haywood, and Al Holbert

1988 962 (HOLBERT RACING)

Engine: Air-cooled 6-cylinder, single turbo by Andial

Displacement: 2994cc

Output: 700 horsepower at 8200rpm

Gearbox: 5-speed manual

Chassis: Aluminum monocoque 2-seat coupe with mid-mounted engine

Performance: Not available

all formed the spearhead of what became a formidable winning machine. From 1983, Porsche produced a batch of cars for sale to race customers and very soon the 956 was the race car everybody wanted to drive in any serious sports car race series.

Porsche could not ignore the opportunity to race in its most important expert market. In 1984, the 956 had to be modified by extending its wheelbase ahead of the front axle line to comply with the regulations for the lucrative Camel-sponsored IMSA sports car series. Called the 962, the new model also replaced the 956 in endurance racing. By 1985, the 962 was

Did You Know?

The Porsche 956/962 is a seven-time Le Mans 24 Hours winner, a five-time winner at the Daytona 24 Hours, and a four-time winner at the Sebring 12 Hours, and is Porsche's most successful race car family of all time.

racing in every major sports car series in the world.

The demands of the IMSA series transformed the 962. With development driven by Porsche's motorsport representative in the United States, Al Holbert, the 962 went through a fast-track development to turn it into a competitive sprint racer. Holbert would win more IMSA races than any other driver and won Le Mans three times. Credit for the engine's competitiveness in IMSA goes to the Californian Andial company and Alwin Springer in particular. After Holbert's untimely death in a light plane accident in 1988, Springer ensured the

962 remained a force in IMSA until the late 1980s.

Porsche's defeat by Jaguar at Le Mans in 1988 signaled the end of the 962's reign at the top of endurance racing, and in IMSA the superior tractability of the Nissans and Jaguars eventually dominated in IMSA.

Through the early 1990s, private 962s continued to be the mainstay of sports car racing across the world. The last 962 win in IMSA came as late as 1993—and a year later a Dauer 962 "lookalike" won Le Mans. *Historical photos courtesy porsche AG*

The itch to do a 911 with all-wheel drive had been with Porsche since its introduction in 1964. The opportunity to develop all-wheel drive came in the 1980s with a growing fascination to win perhaps the most grueling off-road rally in the world—the Paris-Dakar. The engineers at Porsche had always included a small group of enthusiastic rally supporters, and the company's history is liberally decorated with highlights in all the major events. 1980s Motorsport department head, Peter Falk, had also co-driven a largely unmodified 911 to a class victory on the famous Monte Carlo Rally in 1965.

The Paris-Dakar was a near-7,500-mile rally that included North African sections running across some of the most inhospitable areas of desert in the world. The rally came to Porsche's attention because their lead race driver Jacky Ickx won the event in 1983 driving a Mercedes truck. Ickx was a big fan of the demanding desert rally-raids—as they were called—and had no difficulty persuading Porsche to enter.

953 was the first desert "raid" 911—a Carrera 3.2 heavily modified with the all-wheel drive, fiberglass panels, and a great deal of strengthening. Engine power was 230 horsepower and without turbocharging—absolute power was a low priority on loose desert surfaces.

1986 953/959 RALLY

Engine: Air-cooled flat 6-cylinder, twin turbo with intercoolers
Displacement: 2849cc
Output: 400 horsepower at 6500rpm
Gearbox: 5-speed manual
Chassis: All-wheel drive, rear engine unitary construction steel bodyshell with 2+2 cabin
Performance: Not available

Did You Know?

Three 959 rally cars were entered on the 1986 Paris-Dakar rally. The third car was driven by technicians Kussmaul and Unger. Despite having to work on the other two cars throughout the event, they still managed to finish sixth!

Factory drivers Rene Metge and Dominic Lemoigne won the event first time out, with Ickx and his co-driver Claude Brasseur finishing sixth. Support engineer Roland Kussmaul, even after working hard to keep the others running, finished seventeenth in the support truck!

The following year saw the debut of the prototype 959—an altogether more sophisticated machine with bodywork including faired-in headlamps and a large rear wing. The engine remained normally aspirated at 230 horsepower, but all the cars retired. In 1986, the team went with two 400 horsepower twin turbo 959s and a full team backup that included a spotter aircraft. With some 500 starters, Metge and Lemoigne eventually won from Ickx and Brasseur. Fewer than 80 cars reached the finish, but Porsche had proven the 959 was as capable a rally car as a street supercar. *Historical photos courtesy Porsche AG*

Porsche's CEO in the mid-1980s was German-born American Peter Schutz. Schutz was decisive about the importance of the 911 to Porsche and also about winning at Le Mans. He set the engineers to work to build the best 911s and to win the big race in the upcoming Group C endurance race formula. And in parallel, he approved Porsche's involvement in a brand-new F1 engine for McLaren. The

1987 2708 INDYCAR

Engine: Liquid-cooled V-8-cylinder, 4 valves per cylinder single turbocharger
Displacement: 2649cc
Output: 720 horsepower at 11800rpm
Gearbox: 5-speed manual
Chassis: Aluminium honeycomb monocoque single-seater
Performance: Not available

TAG turbo V-6 won three consecutive world championships from 1984 to 1986. Nevertheless, Schutz believed the business needed a high-profile motorsport presence in North America. He was influenced strongly in this thinking by the energy and success of his American motorsport representative, Al Holbert. By 1986, Holbert had established the 962 as the car to beat in IMSA and he had Schutz's ear. Porsche

Did You Know?
During the time of the 1986–1990 CART program, Porsche had no fewer than three CEOs. It is perhaps no wonder all involved with the project wondered whether the fates were against them!

began scaling down its interest with McLaren (surely one of the company's great missed opportunities!) and meanwhile began work on designing a brand-new single seater and engine for a planned debut in the 1988 CART series.

Hans Mezger drew out a V-8 turbo engine using much of the technology from the F1 V-6, except the Indy engine used a single large turbo in place of two smaller units. With the help of Motronic electronic ignition, the 1988 engine produced around 720 horsepower—good compared to the opposition.

Much to the disappointment of the Weissach engineers, the V-8 was switched to a new March chassis in place of their own, but still the results failed to come. The project was dealt a double

blow with the retirement of development director Helmuth Bott and the tragic death of Al Holbert in a plane crash at the end of September. Nevertheless, under the direction of new project leader, the veteran Helmut Flegl, a special car was built by March for 1989, and in the hands of driver Teo Fabi, it won at Mid-Ohio and placed well at most other races.

After some development problems, March delivered a new car for 1990. Unfortunately it proved to be a lemon and Fabi and new teammate John Andretti were unable to record any wins. And by this time a new CEO was advocating a (disastrous) change from CART to Formula One. *Photos courtesy Porsche AG*

The 944 Turbo Cup started the Porsche one-model race series ball rolling in 1986. But as Porsche's general sales stumbled in the late 1980s, it was clear that the race series should be marketing the capabilities of the principal model—the 911. The new 964 all-wheel-drive model was ready for production in late 1988, and the decision was made to develop a special production-based 911 to take over from the 944 Turbo.

1990 PORSCHE 911 CARRERA (964) CUP

Engine: Air-cooled flat 6-cylinder, overhead camshafts, 2 valves per cylinder

Displacement: 3600cc

Output: 270 horsepower at 6100rpm

Gearbox: 5-speed manual

Chassis: Rear engine, rear wheel drive unitary construction steel bodyshell with 2+2 cabin

Performance: Not available

Under the guidance of leading engineers Helmut Flegl and Roland Kussmaul, and working within very limited modification guidelines, a 964 was stripped, re-manufactured, and re-assembled into a race car. It was a tried and tested formula, with all the soundproofing and unnecessary equipment (including the power steering, but not the ABS) removed, a more powerful braking system installed, stiffer and lower suspension, and carefully built

engines. In fact, the first Carrera Cup cars had the pick of the best production engines. While the regular 964 production maximum power was 250 horsepower, the 50 Carrera Cup 911s built for the first year delivered around 270 horsepower. The series launched in 1990 in Germany only, but was over-subscribed. Close racing was the attraction, combined with appearances of "celebrity" drivers and, of course, the 911s made a lot more noise than the 944s! The cars were strictly controlled by Porsche with sealed ECUs and other key engine parts. Interest from around the world was immediate.

In 1993 the series became the Porsche Supercup, and the races supported seven F1 grands prix events. For the first time, Carrera Cup series were promoted in France and Japan also. Supercup went from strength to strength and grew in status worldwide, supporting most of the F1 grands prix wherever they appeared. The cars themselves evolved year on year, becoming first 993-based in 1994 and 996 GT–based in 1998 (a useful pre-test for the 1999 GT3 model).

The 964 Cup had proven to be a critical catalyst for Porsche's Motorsport department at a time when it was pressured not only by falling production sales but also as a way of finding a new direction after a period of considerable uncertainty. *Photos courtesy Porsche AG*

By the mid-1990s, endurance racing had experienced another of its cyclical mood swings and veered away from pure prototypes to cars that at least gave the impression they were derived from street models. In 1995, Le Mans had been won by a McLaren GTR, a full coupe and derived from a very limited production supercar. In 1996, Porsche decided they would produce their own supercar coupe in the form

1998 PORSCHE 911 GT1-98

Engine: Liquid-cooled flat 6-cylinder, 4 valves per cylinder, twin intercooled turbos

Displacement: 3200cc

Output: 550 horsepower at 7200rpm

Gearbox: 6-speed manual with sequential selection

Chassis: Mid-engine, rear wheel drive carbon fiber monocoque coupe

Performance: Not available

of the 911 GT1, a fully modified supercar based on the then current 993 production 911. This didn't go as far as the almost full prototype that was the 1978 935-78—the Moby Dick—but it did push the envelope of what was considered an acceptable GT1 race car—including its 600 horsepower twin turbo flat-6.

But 1996 didn't quite go according to plan. At Le Mans Porsche came up against the

prototype that had been designed, built, but never raced by them in 1995. A pair of the Jaguar-derived WSC-95 open spyders were loaned to a top professional race team run by Reinhold Joest. And Joest proceeded to use these cars to beat the 911 GT1s at Le Mans in 1996!

The 1997 version of the GT1 had been handicapped by the regulations in an attempt to maintain the McLaren's competitiveness, but it was the new Mercedes-Benz coupes that proved to be the match of the GT1s in the FIA GT championship. Only Mercedes didn't enter Le Mans in 1997. An updated version of the GT1 called the Evo improved competitiveness, but to the dismay of the Porsche people, the Joest-run WSC-95 won again. The GT1 had been quicker than the prototype, but it retired.

Mercedes did go to Le Mans in 1998, but instead of using their 6-liter V-12 CLK-GTRs that were so dominant in the FIA championship, they ran a pair of V-8–engined cars. Toyota also was very competitive with a brand-new GT1 "prototype" that owed more to an F1 car. Porsche ran the all-new GT1-98— complete with full carbon fiber chassis and only a vestigial resemblance to a street 911. The two factory cars finished 1–2 after a very hard race.
Historical photos courtesy Porsche AG

The RS Spyder was an all-new endurance race prototype and marked the end of a prominent gap in the company's high-profile motorsport history that had existed since the GT1-98 program was stopped in 1998. Nevertheless, from a public viewpoint this was still a low-profile effort as Porsche decided not to compete in the top class.

The car was constructed to the Le Mans Prototype Category 2 regulations (LMP2) with the intention of competing in the high-profile American Le Mans Series (ALMS) from 2005. The car was notable for its state-of-the-art carbon fiber chassis and an all-new 3.4-liter V-8 normally aspirated gasoline engine. The engine and 6-speed electro-pneumatic

2008 PORSCHE RS SPYDER

Engine: Liquid-cooled V-8, double overhead camshafts, 4 valves per cylinder
Displacement: 3397cc
Output: 476 horsepower (349kW) at 9800rpm
Gearbox: 6-speed sequential manual gearbox
Chassis: Carbon fiber/Kevlar-reinforced monocoque spyder with rear diffuser and rear wing
Performance: Not available

sequential gearbox were rigidly attached to the chassis and acted as stressed components, with the rear suspension mounted off the gearbox casing. Suspension all around used a pushrod arrangement with compact torsion bar springs.

The car was given a thorough redevelopment for 2008 with revised aerodynamics and a reworked engine optimized to run on the ALMS prescription fuel, which included 10% bio-ethanol. Maximum engine power remained under 500 horsepower, despite a 42.9mm diameter restrictor on the intake duct.

The factory cars were entered by Penske Racing—a name steeped in nostalgia for fans of Porsche's adventures in the CanAm Challenge of 30 years past. The RS Spyder won its class the first time out at Laguna Seca in 2005, and the cars won the ALMS LMP2 class from 2006 to 2008. In the 2007 season, the RS Spyders won their class on 11 out of 12 occasions, with 8 overall victories. Despite a lack of interest from the factory, private teams entered Le Mans and there were class wins in 2008 and 2009. The Le Mans regulations ruled out the RS Spyder for 2010, and reduced factory involvement saw the Cytosport Spyders just beaten into second place in the ALMS championship by the ever-improving Acuras. *Photos courtesy Porsche AG*

Did You Know?

The RS Spyder's most important victory came in 2008 when a Penske Racing entry won the Sebring 12 Hours—the first time the event had been won by a car from a junior class in 24 years.

CHAPTER 8
AIR-COOLED CRESCENDO

The early 1990s were almost disastrous in trading terms for Porsche. The combination of a worldwide recession, poor leadership, and a slow response to increasing Pacific Rim competition ensured production and car sales were very poor at a time when the company could afford it least. However, there was an unshakable quality and experience in the body of engineers working at the research and development center in Weissach. There were several landmark Porsches that emerged in the company's darkest days to act as beacons for the future. Notable among these were the 1991 Carrera RS and the 1993 Turbo 3.6—both 964-model 911s.

There was a lot of internal competition to work on the racy new common platform product developments initiated by new CEO Wendelin Wiedeking from 1992, but those tasked with filling in the space with the development of the "interim" 993 before the new-generation models launched from late 1996 had no lesser a task.

Perhaps the interim tag given to the 993 by the senior management stressed the older, more experienced engineers, but within Weissach there was an understanding that this was the last of the line for the traditional air-cooled Porsche. What they delivered was undoubtedly a best ever 911—and it turned the business around almost overnight.

The degree of modification to the 964 was fairly heavily restricted, but the changes transformed the appeal of the car. The 993 Carrera model flew out of the showrooms from its first arrival in late 1993 and kept selling hard until the line was finally closed at the end of the 1997 model year. That was fortunate because the tired concepts of the 968 and 928 had finally been discontinued in 1995—in part to make way for the rebuilt production operations required for the new generation, but also because they simply weren't selling in any realistic volumes.

It was inevitable that the 993 turbo version would find its own unique position as the flagship of the outgoing breed. Far from being a revamp of what had gone before, the new Turbo gained all-wheel drive and twin turbos—making it the most refined and fastest Turbo to date.

Porsche was about to step into a brave new world with the 996 and Boxster, but in the mid-1990s, the story was all about the 993.

AIR-COOLED CRESCENDO

The Carrera Cup 964 that had launched with the Carrera 2 in 1990 was a stroke of mastery on how to modify a street car for competition. Its creators, the hugely experienced Helmut Flegl and Roland Kussmaul, applied the well-proven Porsche mantra of stripping out everything that wasn't essential, tuning the suspension and brakes, and ensuring they had the best of the new 3.6-liter engines emerging from the Zuffenhausen production line. The

1991 911 CARRERA RS

Engine: Air-cooled flat 6-cylinder with 2 spark plugs per cylinder

Displacement: 3600cc

Output: 260 horsepower (190kW) at 6100rpm

Gearbox: 5-speed manual

Chassis: Rear engine, rear wheel drive unitary construction steel bodyshell with 2+2 cabin

Performance: Maximum speed: 162 mph; 0–62mph in 5.3 seconds

Carrera Cup was an instant and huge success, and as fortune would have it, the decision to focus its production and motorsport interest on the 911 rather than the previous 944 Turbo was inspired.

The worldwide economic recession and ill-thought regulation changes effectively killed off endurance racing with prototypes, but there was still customer demand for a solid, reliable production GT. To qualify the 964 in this type

OW 156

of racing, a limited edition street version of the Carrera Cup car evolved.

The Carrera RS took many in the motoring world by surprise and shocked some—those who were expecting some kind of easy riding sports car were disappointed by its harsh ride and lack of equipment. But using exactly the same equipment formula as the 1973 RS, the 964 version offered Touring and Sport versions to go with more extreme R versions. Common to all were blueprinted engines delivering a maximum power of at least 260 horsepower (190kW), seam welded, non-insulated bodyshell, and solid bushed, modified suspension that gave a ride height of 1.6 inches (40mm) lower. There was a special lightweight wiring harness, limited slip differential, single mass flywheel (Sport only), and higher ratios for first and second gear. Out went the power steering and airbags but ABS was retained. The RS ran on magnesium alloy "Cup" design 17-inch alloys that alone saved 22 lbs (10 kg). In the Touring, the cabin was equipped to the same level as the C2, but excluding such things as air conditioning and even a radio! On the Sport, the equipment was minimal, with signature pull-strap door cards, roll-up window lifters, and simple carpeting in place of the rear seats. The Sports weight was 2690 lbs (1220 kg), 287 lbs (130 kg) lighter than the regular C2. This 911 fully deserved its RS title.

The 911 Turbo had traveled a long way between its launch in late 1974 and 1993, but the fundamental specification and layout of the car was essentially the same. The simple formula of putting a single large turbocharger on the evergreen air-cooled flat six was still a recipe for stunning performance. The engine itself had progressed almost beyond imagination—*evolved* is a more correct description. That first 1970s Turbo delivered just 260 horsepower (190kW) from its 3 liters, but the 1993 version had an extra 600cc, and delivered a full boost 360 horsepower (264kW) shove in the back. The crankcase, crankshaft, rods, and cylinders all came from

1993 PORSCHE 911 TURBO 3.6

Engine: Air-cooled flat-6, 2 valves per cylinder, single turbocharger
Displacement: 3600cc
Output: 360 horsepower at 5500rpm
Gearbox: 5-speed manual
Chassis: Rear engine, rear wheel drive unitary construction steel bodyshell with 2+2 cabin
Performance: Maximum speed: 175mph; 0–62mph in 4.8 seconds

the 964 Carrera 2, but the heads each used just one spark plug, and unlike the Carreras, the previous ignition system was retained with Bosch K-Jetronic injection.

The new turbo engine delivered end-of-era performance. The power was spectacular, and thanks to that single large turbo, it all came in a rush above 3500 rpm. This was a fairground-style ride that ensured the Turbo remained Porsche's flagship sports car.

In the more refined 964 bodyshell, the Turbo experience was much better. Equipped with pulse racing rear-wheel drive only, the new coil spring suspension made for a (slightly) more accommodating ride, and when combined with features such as power steering and ABS, the car was easier to handle. What completed the Turbo 3.6's looks were its low-profile, three-piece Cup Style Speedline alloys—a perfect finish to the signature wide fenders, tea-tray rear wing, and front chin spoilers.

The real significance of the 964-bodied 911 Turbo was that it was the end of an era when raw performance was the main selling point of a Porsche sports car. Insane as it may sound today, this car's attraction to Porsche drivers was that it was so difficult to drive fast.

A lot changed at Porsche in the early 1990s, and this Turbo exemplified what we were about to lose.

Did You Know?

The Turbo 3.6 was the last single-turbo, rear-wheel-drive 911, and marked the end of an era at Porsche for the raw sports car.

It is fortunate indeed that the 993 was an instant success. Porsche desperately needed a winner in 1993—a year when rumors of a takeover were constant, staff numbers were reduced by 15%, and production volumes dipped to just 12,500 cars.

The 993 developed the ideas that had begun on the 964 and took them a lot further. Whereas the bodyshell changes to the 964 had been restricted for cost reasons to below the bumper line, the stylists were given far

1997 PORSCHE 911 CARRERA 4S (993)

Engine: Air-cooled 6-cylinder, 2 valves per cylinder, Motronic engine management

Displacement: 3600cc

Output: 285 horsepower at 6100rpm

Gearbox: 6-speed manual

Chassis: Rear engine, all-wheel drive, unitary construction steel 2+2 bodyshell

Performance: Maximum speed: 168 mph; 0–62 mph in 5.3 seconds

wider flexibility to update the lines of the now 30-year-old classic. British designer Tony Hatter is credited with the transformation, which delivered arguably the prettiest 911 of them all (at least since the very first!). But the 993 was fully 80% different than the 964. These weren't detail changes, but included the superb multi-link rear suspension. First seen on the 928, this system replaced the aging semi-trailing arm arrangement and gave the 993 significantly improved ride and handling. The 3.6-liter

engine used the latest Bosch Motronic engine management to produce 272 horsepower—up 22 horsepower on the 964 version and with virtually no change in fuel consumption. An

Did You Know?

The 993's position as the last of the air-cooled 911s has given it special status among enthusiasts and ensured its position among the greatest of the 911 models.

improved Carrera followed in 1995, with output enhanced by another 13 horsepower, but with notably improved mid-range torque thanks to a variable intake ducting system called Varioram.

To maximize its income from the 993's popularity, Porsche was not slow to bring out as many different model options as possible. The model was launched in coupe and cabriolet versions of the Carrera 2, and in late 1994 these were joined by a Carrera 4 that used an all-new transmission: it was around 50% lighter than the 964's "first cut" system. Equally innovative was the new Targa, featuring a panoramic glass roof that could slide back electrically. The old Targa concept had been long overdue for a remake and the new 993 version reinvented the concept of a 911 drop-head coupe. An RS version was almost inevitable, which followed in early 1995, although the appeal of the new car was more refined than the focused 964 model. For the 1996 model year, there were also two wide-body versions: the Carrera S used the brakes and suspension of the "narrow body" Carrera, while the higher-specification 4S used the Turbo's brakes and suspension.

We can be excused for including another 911 Turbo here as the 993 version re-invented the concept of Porsche's high-speed flagship. While losing none of the original's mouthwatering ability to accelerate spectacularly, the twin turbo, all-wheel-drive 993 version gained a certain degree of user-friendliness.

Customers had to wait 12 months after the end of the 964-model Turbo, but in the spring of 1995 the wait was rewarded with a remarkable machine that sold like hot cakes from the moment it hit the showrooms. Of course, what really fixed the instant appeal of the new Turbo was the number of irresistible curves in a bodyshell that already had its

1995-1998 PORSCHE 911 TURBO (993)

Engine: Air-cooled flat 6-cylinder, twin turbos and intercooler, Motronic ECU

Displacement: 3600cc

Output: 408 horsepower at 5750rpm

Gearbox: 6-speed manual

Chassis: Rear engine, rear wheel drive, unitary construction steel 2+2 bodyshell

Performance: Maximum speed: 180 mph; 0–62mph in 4.5 seconds

fair share. New 18-inch "Technologie" alloys added to the look. These wheels were fabricated using hubs with "hollow spokes" and were

friction-welded together. Each wheel was 20% lighter than the equivalent "Turbo-look" alloy (these alloys were also fitted to the Carrera 4S model) found on the regular Carrera S models. Another notable feature was the "Big Red" Brembo 4-piston brake calipers working on cross-drilled and ventilated steel rotors. The "Big Red" set-up had first been used on the 1993 964 Turbos, and with an ever-improving 4-channel ABS system, gave the 993 Turbo braking ability to match its speed.

All-wheel drive was potentially a hard sell to customers used to the older models, but the 50% lighter system (than seen on the 964 Carreras) gave the 993 model Turbo a new degree of confidence. four hundred eight horsepower is a fierce amount of power and the all-wheel drive gave the car renewed vigor on full boost.

Did You Know?
The most sought-after 993 Turbo is the 450-horsepower Turbo S and the very few that received the Porsche Exclusive (Porsche's own custom brand) 430-horsepower powerkit upgrades. The Turbo S could accelerate from 0 to 62 mph in under 4.1 seconds—0.4 seconds faster than the regular Turbo.

The 993 Turbo remained unchanged in specification until production of air-cooled 911s ended in Zuffenhausen in July 1998. The new 996 model would not be available in Turbo form until 2000, and it was fitting that demand for the last air-cooled Turbo continued with scarcely any reduction long after production of the regular "narrow body" Carreras had ceased.

Today, the 993 Turbo is rightly regarded as an all-time classic, and like so many Turbos before it, a star in the 911 story.

CHAPTER 9
THE NEW GENERATION

There are many who still refer to the water-cooled cars that began to stream out of Porsche from 1996 as the "new" generation. At the time of writing that is over 15 years ago, and today we have another "new" generation emerging that includes the fashionable hybrids as well as the traditional gasoline-powered cars. Nevertheless, the Porsche generation that took over in Zuffenhausen and Weissach in the mid-1990s completely transformed the concept of the Porsche sports car, and what they produced was revolutionary. In business terms, it was a brilliant re-invention, and Porsche began to make money on a scale that could never have been dreamed of before, even in the good times.

The secret of the success came from the marketing specification that defined the new products as appealing to drivers who wouldn't have normally considered a Porsche. The target customers were those who previously would have driven Mercedes and BMW products, for instance—cars that were easy to live with and drive. The Porsche marketing people had also learned from their predecessors. They understood the importance of having not only a 911 product, but a fast-selling entry-level sports car.

We first saw the concept of that new style aspirational Porsche in 1993, when the Boxster did a brief world tour to gauge market reaction. The response was ecstatic, and Porsche pushed ahead with its plans to launch a two-model family called 911 and Boxster.

Meanwhile, inside Porsche, the best word to describe the changing work structure is "carnage." To describe new CEO Wendelin Wiedeking's restructuring of the business as ruthless is a gross understatement: Wiedeking re-invented all the labor and resource-intensive practices that had evolved in Porsche over more than 40 years of building quality sports cars. He brought in Japanese consultants to redefine the way the cars were designed and built and ensured that production costs on the new models were tightly controlled. This even meant that the two new model families would be nearly identical from the doors forward—one would have a mid-engine roadster layout and the other a classic rear engine 911 layout. But all were cheaper to build than anything Porsche had made before. It cut corners, and with the benefit of hindsight it is clear that quality and reliability could have been considered as more important.

But nobody could doubt the overhaul was a spectacular market and business success.

The bubble burst when Wiedeking stretched Porsche too far. Ever more deeply involved in the financial markets, by 2006–2007 Porsche was positioning itself to take over Volkswagen-Audi. In the process Porsche borrowed heavily and left itself exposed to any reversal in stock market fortunes. When those markets collapsed in 2007, Wiedeking's grand plan crashed and burned. A year later the scenario had reversed. Wiedeking had gone and VW was positioning itself to take over a debt-ridden Porsche. The company that had so fiercely defended its independence through any previous adversity was now suddenly defenseless. As one of many VW satellites, the new future for Porsche after 2008 looked very different from anything that had passed before.

THE NEW GENERATION

If you had a clean sheet of paper to design the ideal 2-seat sports car, you would probably come up with the Boxster. The all-new mid-mounted engine was a water-cooled 4-valve-per-cylinder design with a rear-mounted 5-speed gearbox. The attractive roadster styling—the work of American stylist Grant Larson, who took design cues from the race spyders of the 1950s—included a roomy 2-seat cabin and luggage compartments front and rear.

1996 BOXSTER

Engine: Liquid-cooled boxer 6-cylinder, 4 valves per cylinder with Variocam variable inlet valve timing

Displacement: 2480cc

Output: 204 horsepower at 6000rpm

Gearbox: 5-speed manual or Tiptronic automatic

Chassis: Mid-engine, rear wheel drive, unitary construction steel 2-seat roadster

Performance: Maximum speed: 149 mph; 0-62 mph in 6.9 second

The decision to manufacture the Boxster was made in 1992, and just over 4 four years later the new model launched to huge expectations. The name Boxster came from a combination of the Roadster body style and the boxer 6-cylinder engine—the name was given to a 1993 concept car that tested (successfully) market reaction to the proposed new model.

The production Boxster was somewhat larger than the concept car, but this was forced by the need to incorporate worldwide crash protection and safety requirements. Press reaction to the car was beyond Porsche's wildest dreams, especially reaction to the brand-new 204-horsepower, 2.5-liter water-cooled engine.

Did You Know?
The Boxster was the first Porsche that was known officially by a name, rather than by its internal type number (986).

As a version of the common M96 powerplant family used also on the 996, the engine featured Variocam variable inlet valve timing controlled by the Bosch Motronic engine management. The engine also used state-of-the-art coil on plug sparking units.

The Boxster was so successful that within a year, Porsche was transferring production to a sub-contractor in Finland (although the engines were still built in Zuffenhausen). In 2000, the basic Boxster gained a more powerful 220-horsepower, 2.7-liter engine, and the new Boxster S offered a 3.2-liter version with 252 horsepower and improved brakes and suspension. The slightly dated look was given a facelift for the 2003 model year, when the fragile plastic rear window was replaced with a glass window. The thoroughly reworked (80% new) Type 987 Boxster arrived for the 2005 model year with 245 horsepower engines for the Boxster and 280 horsepower for the S. Boxster sales have shown typical sensitivity to world economic conditions, but some 15 years after its launch the model is still regarded as the benchmark by which other sports roadsters are measured.

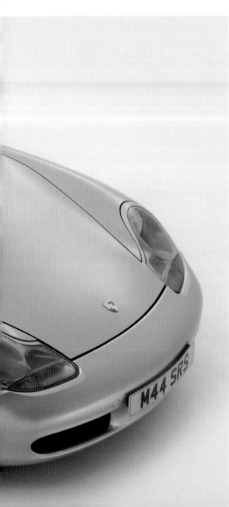

The evergreen Porsche 911 had been in continuous production for 34 years when the "new generation" 911 was introduced in the fall of 1997. But unlike any previous development of the world's best-known sports car, this was a revolutionary, not evolutionary, step forward. This Porsche was designed for maximum revenue generation, and was a "common platform" design with the new Boxster roadster,

PORSCHE 911 CARRERA (996)

Engine: Classic flat-6 cylinder, water-cooled, all alloy with "integrated" wet sump oil system. Bosch Motronic engine management and electronic fuel injection

Displacement: 3.4-liter, rising to 3.6-liter

Output: 300 horsepower rising to 320 horsepower

Gearbox: 6-speed manual or 5-speed Tiptronic auto

Performance: 0–62 mph (manual): 5.2 seconds (facelift 5.0); Maximum speed: 174 mph (facelift 177)

introduced the year before. Indeed, the early 996 was criticized by some for being too similar to its new roommate (they shared largely the same components forward of the doors).

But the new 911 was in a class of its own. It broke with tradition in being water-cooled—a necessary change brought about by the need for a cleaner exhaust and reduced acoustic noise levels. The new engine also allowed the engineers to

E61 FAN

include 4 valves per cylinder and variable timing double overhead camshafts—improvements that gave the first 3.4-liter Carrera models a lively 300 horsepower. The transmission options were as before, with a manual 6-speed gearbox and the impressive Tiptronic auto transmission. Also like before, you could order the Carrera in both traditional rear-wheel drive or with all-wheel drive. Body styles were equally versatile with Coupe, Cabriolet, and Targa options all eventually being offered.

As well as typically impressive performance, the interior was brought into the 1990s with air conditioning that actually worked, an ergonomically sensible switchgear layout, and more usable trunk space. No longer

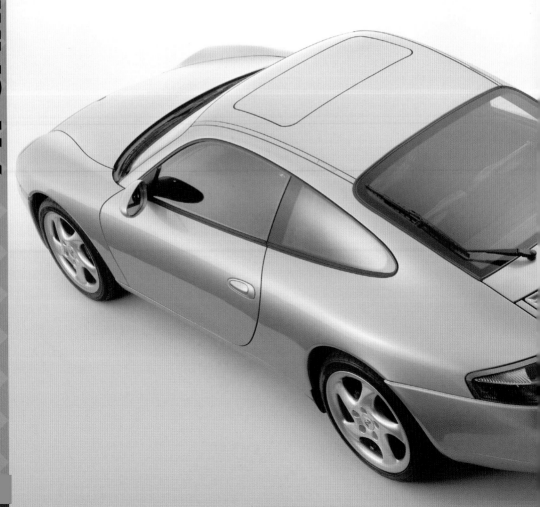

were the 911's ergonomics a source of fun for the automotive press; this was a true grand touring sports car that appealed to all types of performance car buyers, not just the hardened enthusiast.

The 996 was a spectacular sales success for Porsche in the late 1990s, bringing new drivers to Porsche from all the premium brand manufacturers. It was upgraded with the Turbo's headlamps and an extra 20 horsepower for the 2002 model year (these are often called the facelift models), and by the time it was replaced by the 997 in September 2004, some 175,000 had been made, of which around 145,000 were the mainstream Carrera models.

Engine and technical photos courtesy Porsche AG

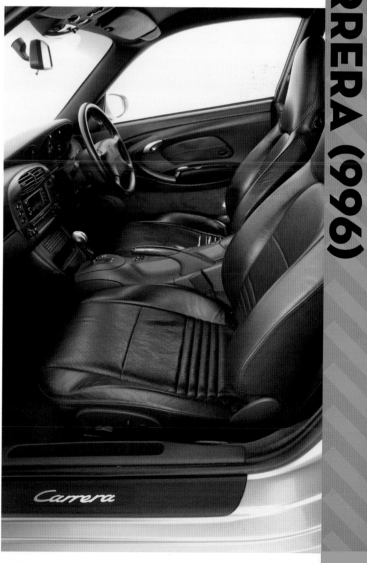

With mainstream 911 production converting to the 996 model from late 1997, it was essential that the Motorsport department adopt the new body style in place of the previous 993-based Cup 911. After various tests, it became clear that it was unsuited to the demands of motorsport. Specifically, the production engine was essentially a wet sump design rather than the previous dry sump and in hard cornering there were serious oil surge problems. The decision to go the "integrated

2000 PORSCHE 911 GT3 (996)

Engine: Liquid-cooled, dry pan flat 6-cylinder, 4 valves per cylinder

Displacement: 3600cc

Output: 360 horsepower at 7200rpm

Gearbox: 6-speed manual

Chassis: Rear engine, rear wheel drive, unitary construction (based on C4) steel bodyshell

Performance: Maximum speed: 188 mph; 0–62mph in 4.8 seconds

oil tank" route in the Carrera's engine for purely cost reasons would prove to be ultimately expensive—a mistake that the 901's original designers had not made 30 years previously.

For motorsport, the proposal was to develop a separate water-cooled engine based on the 993-based GT1 engine design (itself developed from the original 964 engine), with full dry sump oiling and 4-valves per cylinder. The costs of this development were amortized by a far-sighted decision to use the same engine in the future 996 version of the Turbo.

The original 1998 Supercup cars were the responsibility of the hugely experienced Roland Kussmaul, but to gain homologation into the FIA's GT3 championships, a limited edition of street cars was required. One thousand three hundred sixty cars were slotted into Zuffenhausen production schedule at the end of 1999—and the car sold out immediately.

The GT3 had instant street identification thanks to its special bodykit that included a deeper front bumper, sculpted rocker moldings, and an attractive bi-plane rear spoiler. The GT3's bodyshell was based on a modified Carrera 4 shell (this was more rigid than the C2). The suspension was stiffer and lowered 1.2 inches (30mm), while the sway bars were all adjustable. Brakes were 4-piston monobloc (machined from solid) units working on huge cross-drilled 13-inch diameter rotors. An original GT3 can also be identified by its 2-piece 10-spoke alloys. These first-run GT3s also have the attraction of being set up in the Motorsport department after final assembly.

The GT3 series was repeated for 2004, but as a mainstream model with 381 horsepower and using the facelifted shell of the later 996 Carreras. The regular GT3 was also joined by the homologation special GT3 RS.

Did You Know?
The original 996 GT3s were RS models in everything but name, developed just like the 964 RS for a race series (even by the same engineer!) and then produced as a limited edition street model.

The Carrera GT was built to showcase Porsche's expertise in the premium sports car market. Developed from a Le Mans prototype that was in testing before it was summarily cancelled in November 1999, the street car concept was shown at the Paris auto show in September 2000. It represented a clean sheet of paper for the stylists and engineers, but incorporated the 5.5-liter V-10 gasoline race-bred engine, gearbox, and pushrod suspension that had

2003 PORSCHE CARRERA GT

Engine: Liquid-cooled V-10, double overhead camshafts, 4 valves per cylinder with VarioCam

Displacement: 5733cc

Output: 612 horsepower at 8000 rpm

Gearbox: 6-speed manual

Chassis: Mid-engine carbonfiber plastic with carbon/Kevlar-reinforced 2-seat roadster body.

Performance: Maximum speed: 205 mph; 0–62mph in 3.9 seconds

been developed for the new Le Mans racer. These key motorsport components ensured the specification of the Carrera GT was at the highest level.

The mid-mounted V-10 engine was detuned to 612 horsepower and made quieter by using camshaft drive chains rather than gears. Variocam variable inlet valve timing was incorporated, and the 6-speed, transverse, hydraulically shifted gearbox was converted from the sequential system used on the race car to a conventional gate. Race technology carried over to the production chassis, which was carbon-fiber-reinforced plastic. This was a sandwich comprising the main chassis tub and a top section including the windscreen frame

Did You Know?

The gearknob on the Carrera GT is made from beech wood, echoing the 1960s race cars that had light wood gearknobs for weight saving.

and rollover bars. Both the brakes and the twin-disc clutch were ceramic, with the front brakes using 6-piston calipers.

In its styling, the Carrera GT was allowed to break free of the legacy requirements that governed most other production Porsches. Styling head Harm Lagaay, and the experienced Grant Larson, developed a roadster body style that was instantly Porsche. Inevitably the car was covered in large inlet ducts for the big V-10, but the real revelation was the interior. This was a completely clean sheet design for a Porsche and featured a large central tunnel to separate driver and passenger.

Starting off in the Carrera GT required a special launch procedure, thanks to the very small diameter twin plate ceramic clutch and the need for engine revs to prevent stalling. Nevertheless, on the move the performance was electrifying. The only slight disappointment was the slightly strangled sound made by the V-10!

Despite good economic conditions in the early 2000s, Porsche was extremely cagey about how many Carrera GTs would be made at the new Leipzig facility. With a price tag of $440,000, production began in late 2003 and just 1,270 cars were sold—less than had been hoped for originally.

The Cayman is arguably the prettiest modern Porsche. Forever dubbed by the media as the Boxster hard-top, Porsche has always tried to position the Cayman away from (or, rather, above) its soft-top brother. From its launch in late 2005 for the 2006 model year, the Cayman received slightly more powerful engines than the Boxster. The Cayman S, for instance, had a maximum power of 295 horsepower compared to the Boxster S having 280 horsepower. From 2007 they shared powerplants, which was always going to be to the benefit of the roadster.

There have been several interesting Cayman S special editions. The first was the 2008 Design Edition 1. The 777 cars were in black with black

interiors and 19-inch Turbo alloys. The Cayman S Sport was also announced in 2008 and used the 303 horsepower engine from the Boxster

2009 PORSCHE CAYMAN S

Engine: Liquid-cooled 6-cylinder, double overhead camshafts, 4 valves per cylinder

Displacement: 3387cc

Output: 320 horsepower at 7200rpm

Gearbox: 6-speed manual or 7-speed PDK automatic

Chassis: Mid-engine, rear wheel drive, 2-seat unitary construction steel coupé

Performance: Maximum speed: 171mph; 0–62mph in 5.4 seconds

Design Edition 1. These cars came in either orange or bright green, but could be ordered in more conventional colors. They had a dash plaque to identify the limited edition of 700.

The Cayman is the enthusiast's choice because, combined with its desirable mid-engine layout, its chassis stiffness is almost identical to the 997 coupe and nearly 2.5 times stiffer than the Boxster. Combine the superbly balanced handling and braking with a 300 horsepower engine and, from 2009, the impressive PDK dual clutch gearbox, and the Cayman S adds up to a serious package. It also has some useful practical advantages in being quieter in the cabin and having larger storage space.

Caymans have been mostly built alongside the Boxster in Uuisikaupunki in Finland by the sub-contract company Valmet Automotive. This explains the "U" at the 10th digit of the Vehicle Identification Number (if you have an "S" there your car was built in Stuttgart). From

Did You Know?

The 320-horsepower Cayman S enjoys more maximum power than the spectacular 964-bodied Carrera RS and the same power as the widely acclaimed 964 model 911 Turbo.

2012, and with Porsche AG now managed by Volkswagen, Boxster/Cayman transferred to the newly reopened ex-Karmann factory in Osnabrück in Germany.

The Cayman has always struggled in the marketplace, not least because buyers have difficulty in understanding the price premium compared to the Boxster. This reduced volume, compared to the Boxster, will surely give the car exclusivity later in its life as an emerging Porsche classic.

After seven years of unbroken success in the marketplace with the 996 model, the 997 refreshed interest in Porsche's modern 911. While the look was updated considerably (and made a stronger link with earlier classic 911s), there was also a considerable performance uplift. The Carreras were offered in two forms—the 325-horsepower 3.6-liter and the 355 horsepower 3.8-liter S. All were available in coupe and cabriolet body styles and with the option of manual or Tiptronic gearboxes. The cars were

2006 PORSCHE 911 CARRERA S (997)

Engine: Liquid-cooled 6-cylinder, double overhead camshafts, 4 valves per cylinder

Displacement: 3824cc

Output: 355 horsepower at 6600 rpm

Gearbox: 6-speed manual or 5-speed Tiptronic

Chassis: Rear engine, rear wheel drive, unitary construction steel 2+2 bodyshell

Performance: Maximum speed: 179 mph; 0–62mph in 4.8 seconds

more slippery than the 996, and alongside the various changes to improve crash safety in the bodyshell, there was an 8% increase in bodyshell stiffness. The coupe is around 110 lb (50 kg) heavier than the equivalent 996, but the increase in engine power more than makes up for this.

The interior was also completely redesigned with many more options available for seating comfort. This was also the first 911 not to have an emergency wheel of some kind. In the event of a puncture, the driver injects a sealant into

Did You Know?
Despite the Gen 2 997 Carrera S having an 8.5% increase in maximum power and being nearly 10% quicker to 62 mph from standstill over the Gen 1 997S model, the later car uses nearly 7% less gasoline and releases 9% less carbon dioxide emissions on a standard duty cycle.

the tire, reinflates it, and drives to the nearest tire depot.

Perhaps controversially, the service intervals for the 2004 models (the last year of the 996) had been increased to 20,000 miles or 2 years (whichever came sooner). While paralleling industry fashions, the long service intervals would prove problematic for some on this high-performance sports car, particularly when used constantly from short urban journeys.

For 2007, a 997-model Turbo arrived with Variable Turbine Geometry in the turbos and trademark sensational performance. A less aggressive driver that year was the new targa, although oddly this was only available on the all-wheel-drive cars.

The second generation 997s followed for the 2009 model year, and these cars could be identified by their daytime running lights. The cars featured small improvements to the front and rear bumpers, but under the skin was a new direct fuel injection engine (still a flat-6 of course) with better power, economy, and exhaust emissions. The "Gen 2" Carrera delivered an impressive maximum power of 345 horsepower (253kW), while the Carrera S models had 385 horsepower (282kW). The winning new feature on the Gen 2 cars was undoubtedly the new PDK gearbox.

The 997 Carrera models were progressively replaced by the new 991 model 911 from late 2011.

911 CARRERA (997)

CHAPTER 10
THE NEW DIRECTION

The history of Porsche includes several stories of how the company clawed its way back from the brink of bankruptcy when economic times were hard. The mid-1970s, early 1980s, and early 1990s were difficult times for an independent sports car company with a product mix that was undeniably dominated by a single model—the 911. Throughout its history, Porsche's managers have tried hard to break away from the dependency on the 911 and have produced some great sports cars as a result. Think of the 912, 914, the 924, and 944, and most recently, the Boxster. All played their part in boosting sales—but generally only when the world's economies were healthy.

In the middle of the severe business slump of the early 1990s, the whirlwind that was Dr. Wendelin Wiedeking had to grasp and understand Porsche's vulnerabilities very quickly. His first task after he was placed in charge of the day-to-day business from 1992 was to save Porsche from bankruptcy. This was a necessarily brutal process, but Porsche recovered and emerged in the late 1990s with two very good product families that enjoyed many common parts and processes. The cars were much cheaper to make, cost less, and fortunately, they sold like no other Porsches had.

With the 996 and Boxster firmly established, Wiedeking turned his attentions to enlarging the product line by introducing completely new models that were outside the traditional sports car types, but from which Porsche could benefit by virtue of its strong brand image. The first studies looked into the possibility of either a people carrier/minivan (MPV) or a sport utility vehicle (SUV). The SUV idea was one that had been close to Ferry Porsche's heart in the 1970s, but the family's departure from the management board meant the idea didn't progress for several decades. Wiedeking came very close to agreeing to terms for a new joint venture SUV with Mercedes in the late 1990s, but eventually Porsche signed a cost-sharing development with Volkswagen for a common platform SUV.

The Porsche SUV—named the Cayenne in 2000—would set a trend for 'out-of-box' developments initiated by Dr. Wiedeking. From its launch in 2003, the Cayenne proved to be a success in many markets and exceeded the manufacturer's expectations. And given confidence by that success, Porsche began to look at a fourth model family using the powertrain developed for the SUV. The Panamera arrived in 2008 and added a luxury grand touring car to the Porsche model lineup.

Parallel to this aggressive model development strategy, the large profits and associated stock market value increases of the Porsche business seduced those at the top of Porsche into believing the company could take over the significantly larger Volkswagen-Audi group. As a way of raising capital for activities in this area, the business took various substantial loans. Unfortunately, in 2007, the financial markets turned in such a way that the loan interest payments overwhelmed the regular business'

cash flow. The sudden financial crisis brought about Dr. Wiedeking's departure and the company fell easily into the hands of VW-Audi. The loss of Porsche's independence, fiercely defended in earlier years, resulted in a complete culture change in Zuffenhausen. Subsequently, Porsche development has appeared to focus on new era forms of propulsion, while the Cayenne and Panamera models each received VW diesel engines—which would have been considered an impossible option for a Porsche just 10 years earlier.

From 2008, a stream of concept cars and workable production hybrids began to emerge. Cars driven by hybrid gasoline/electric may be a stepping stone toward new future personal transport systems, and as VW's focus for such development, Porsche has been placed at the forefront of such developments for the group. The new generation forms of propulsion are still in their early stages—particularly the dependency on battery packs. Never slow to benefit from its significant heritage to boost its modern products, Porsche pointed to groundbreaking development of a hybrid vehicle by Ferdinand Porsche in 1900 to demonstrate its previous interest in this area.

The Cayenne family of cars was a complete change and demonstrated more than any other strategy Dr. Wiedeking's plans to take Porsche away from dependency on a limited number of sports car products. The SUV was a very big commitment for the business—and its customers—to swallow. This was a joint development shared (financially) by VW and Porsche, even though it was predominantly a Porsche design team that developed the core components of the chassis.

2003 PORSCHE CAYENNE TURBO

Engine: Liquid-cooled V-8, double overhead camshafts, 4 valves per cylinder
Displacement: 4511cc
Output: 450 horsepower at 6000rpm
Gearbox: 6-speed Tiptronic automatic
Chassis: Front engine, all-wheel drive, unitary construction steel bodyshell with 5 seats
Performance: Maximum speed: 165 mph; 0–62mph in 5.6 seconds

A brand-new factory was built in Leipzig to be the hub of Cayenne production.

The Cayenne launched to great fanfare in late 2002 (2003 in the United States) with two variants being offered—the Cayenne S and the Cayenne Turbo. Both were powered by a brand-new Porsche-designed 4.5-liter V-8, with the base version delivering a healthy 320 horsepower, and the Turbo enjoying twin turbochargers to develop a maximum 450 horsepower. Both models came with 6-speed

Tiptronic transmission and permanent all-wheel drive, and the Cayenne S used coil spring suspension with permanent all-wheel drive. Also (but standard on the Turbo), air suspension that could be adjusted for ride height and automatically compensated for loading was available. The Cayenne offered sophisticated off-road adjustability to allow the car to ford streams and negotiate steep muddy slopes (although the reality was that very few Cayennes would ever see such conditions). The bottom line was that this was as hi-tech as an off-road vehicle could be. Equipment levels inside were high, with full leather interiors and climate control. If it all sounds good so far, the problem that most picked up on straight away was the appearance. Wide rear quarters gave the car an ungainly look that wasn't addressed until a model facelift in early 2007. Nevertheless, in Porsche's most important export market—the United States—the Cayenne sold well, and the target of 25,000 cars a year was quickly achieved from the new assembly plant in Leipzig.

Did You Know?

The Cayenne Turbo's air suspension (an option on the S) allows the ride height to be increased to fully 22 inches (555mm) in the special off-road mode and it can cross water up to that deep also—the bodyshell is sealed to prevent any water from finding its way in.

2004 saw a third model added to the family, called simply Cayenne. Powered by a 250-horsepower, 3.2-liter V-6, it addressed the growing negative sentiment in Europe toward large, gas-guzzling cars and became a strong seller, leading the way for the Cayenne Diesel, introduced in Europe only in May 2009. The Diesel represented a very brave step by a company renowned for its high-performance sports cars, and in 2010, Porsche even began offering a hybrid version of the popular Cayenne. *Photos courtesy Porsche AG*

The Panamera broke cover in the fall of 2008 and at first look appears to be the 4-seater model that so nearly made it to the market back in 1992—the 989. The 989 was a 3.5-liter V-8 grand touring car with four doors that looked similar in concept. The 989 was cancelled because at that time Porsche was virtually bankrupt and a high-end GT was the last model they needed. The idea never completely died, and 10 years later studies began again as soon as the Cayenne was in production. It was important to Dr. Wiedeking to have as many model lines in his product mix as possible to reduce the company's cash flow sensitivity to economic slowdowns. Unfortunately, such a slowdown happened in 2007, and the new Panamera nearly fell victim to the financial crisis brought about by over-extending the company in the financial markets. But this time, and unlike the 989, the new car made it into production with a modest target of just 20,000 cars in the first year.

Did You Know?

The Panamera hybrid can run at up to 85 mph on full electric power, with an electric-only range of 2 kilometers (1.24 miles).

2009 PANAMERA S

Engine: Liquid-cooled V-8, VariCam Plus with Direct Fuel Injection
Displacement: 4806cc
Output: 400 horsepower (294kW) at 6500rpm
Gearbox: 6-speed manual or 7-speed PDK automatic
Chassis: Front engine, rear wheel drive, unitary construction steel 4-seat bodyshell
Performance: Maximum speed: 177 mph; 0–62mph in 5.6 seconds (5.4s with PDK)

It is a startling car—very large in comparison to the company's sports cars—but there is no doubting its sumptuous presentation and high technical specification. The range was launched with three models—S, 4S and Turbo—followed subsequently by a V-6–powered hybrid and a diesel model. The core engine is the 4.8-liter V-8 with direct fuel injection (DFI) and VarioCam Plus variable valve adjustment. The car bristles with leading-edge automotive technology, including the 7-speed PDK transmission and Porsche Active Stability Management (PASM) active suspension. The Panamera hybrid is the first full hybrid in the luxury car segment, powered by a 3.6-liter V6 derived from the full V-8. The parallel hybrid system is as developed as that of the Cayenne hybrid. The value of this system comes in reducing overall gasoline consumption, particularly when cruising on highways. There's even talk of a 2-door coupe— now that would really please fans of the old 928!

Photos courtesy Porsche AG

How things change. This writer remembers interviewing Porsche's Research and Development VP Horst Marchart back in the early 1990s and being told there would never be a diesel in the Porsche lineup (I recall his comment "think of that 'clack-clack' noise, just like a truck!"). But some 15 years later everything has changed—in Porsche and in the perception the world has of the automobile. In Europe today, diesels probably outnumber

2009 CAYENNE DIESEL

Engine: Liquid-cooled V-6, common rail fuel injection with single VTG turbo, twin intercoolers

Displacement: 2967cc

Output: 240 horsepower at 4000rpm

Gearbox: 8-speed Tiptronic automatic

Chassis: Front engine, all wheel drive, unitary construction steel bodyshell

Performance: Maximum speed: 133 mph; 0–62mph in 8.3 seconds

gasoline-powered vehicles—mainly because in some countries diesel is much cheaper, but also because fuel consumption on the high-efficiency oil burners has become a fine art. A typical VW Golf mid-size car can match a Toyota Prius for fuel consumption. VW is perhaps the undisputed leaders in diesel fuel engine technology, and given the new directions Porsche has taken since 2009, when the VW-Audi empire began to flex its muscles over the company, it was inevitable a diesel would find its way onto a Porsche car. The engines are far more efficient, and they simply don't sound like they used to either. In countries where diesel is cheap, it is an essential part of any premium auto manufacturer's product mix—and Porsche had to be there to be taken seriously.

The engine is an Audi (inevitably) 3-liter V-6 with 240 horsepower—a state-of-the-art 4-valve-per-cylinder, double overhead camshaft unit with common rail injection, a single turbo (with Variable Turbine Geometry), and two intercoolers. The engine drives through an 8-speed Tiptronic transmission and has the fairly modest (but easy to maintain) mechanical suspension. It is clear that the car is aimed at Main Street/school run users. But it is an attractive proposition in terms of the cabin and upscaled appearance of the modern Cayenne. The turbo suppresses an already well damped diesel "clatter" and even with Tiptronic, the car runs from 0 to 62 mph in just 8.3 seconds.

Did You Know?

One tank of diesel fuel in the Cayenne can carry it at least 600 miles (over 1000kms), with combined CO2 emissions of 195g/km—equivalent to most faster mid-size cars.

Porsche first declared interest in developing hybrid technology in late 2004, when news leaked that it had opened discussions with Japanese manufacturer Toyota. Toyota was among the accepted leaders in parallel technology hybrid vehicles, and by this time had just released its own hybrid SUV (the RX400h). Nevertheless, such was the newness of this technology to Porsche, it wasn't until November 2007 that a Cayenne Hybrid prototype was shown (at the Los Angeles auto show). It would be 2010 before the

2009 CAYENNE S HYBRID

Engine: Liquid-cooled V-8, double overhead camshafts, 4 valves per cylinder
Displacement: 2995cc
Output: V6: 333 horsepower (245kW) from 5500 to 6500rpm; (Electric): 47 horsepower (34kW) from 1150rpm
Gearbox: 8-speed Tiptronic
Chassis: Front engine, all wheel drive, unitary construction steel bodyshell
Performance: Maximum speed: 150 mph; 0–62mph in 6.5 seconds

1. High voltage nickel-metal hydride battery
2. Air supply duct
3. Power electronics
4. Hybrid module
5. 3,0-Liter V6 compressor engine

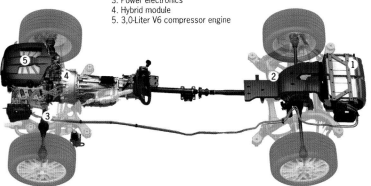

first production Porsche hybrid appeared on the market.

The Cayenne hybrid uses a direct (gasoline) fuel-injected, supercharged Audi-based V-6 developing 333 horsepower as its main powerplant, working with a 47 horsepower (34kW) electric motor. Porsche claims the same level of performance as the Cayenne S with CO_2 emissions less than 200g/km and fuel consumption under 8.4 liters/100km (34.4 mpg) to the New European Driving Cycle (NEDC) combined test. This compares to the Cayenne S similar test result of 10.5 l/100km (26.9 mpg), which suggests a 28% improvement in gas consumption.

Did You Know?

The hybrid is heavy, with a curb weight of 4939 lbs (2240 kg) making it the heaviest production Porsche ever, but the benchmark performance acceleration to 62 mph is still impressive at 6.5 seconds (against the Cayenne S 5.9 seconds).

The two power units in the Cayenne Hybrid are connected by a separator clutch controlled by what Porsche calls a Hybrid Manager. This can sequence the drive from the V6, the electric motor, or both. The system includes a 288-volt Nickel Metal Hydride battery pack fitted under the rear load area. The battery pack stores energy when braking and driving under normal conditions. The Hybrid Manager also has the facility to improve fuel consumption at highway speeds by "sailing"—at speeds up to 97 mph, the electric motor can take over completely (shutting the engine down) when drive power is not required, improving fuel consumption. As soon as the driver presses the accelerator pedal the engine restarts and increased power is available (for overtaking, for instance).

The limitations of Porsche's first hybrid may be obvious, but this is clearly an area of development that is going to make huge advances very quickly. Meanwhile the Cayenne Hybrid (and the Panamera Hybrid) are helping reduce the "gas guzzler" image that big V-8–engined cars might otherwise have. *Photos courtesy Porsche AG*

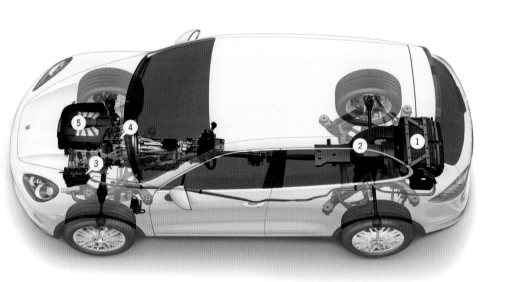

1. High voltage nickel-metal hydride battery
2. Air supply duct
3. Power electronics
4. Hybrid module
5. 3.0-liter V6 compressor engine

The importance of the 2010 918 Spyder is that as Porsche's first hybrid sports car concept, it is at the cutting edge of the company's strategy to develop cars that combine a gasoline engine power source with electric motive power. The layout of the carbon-fiber composite spyder is fairly conventional in having a mid-mounted, 500 horsepower, 3.2-liter V-8 engine. Derived from the engine used in the LMP2 RS Spyder race car, the powerplant drives through a 6-speed PDK gearbox to give the conventionally powered car a maximum speed of nearly 200 mph and 94 mph on electric power. The concept car is what is called a "plug-in hybrid" where the conventional engine also drives a generator that charges a Lithium-ion battery pack behind the seats. The batteries drive electric motors on the front and rear axles, and these alone produce some 218 horsepower. Range on electric power is just 15.5 miles, but acceleration to 62 mph from standstill is 3.2 seconds. Porsche claims the 918 Spyder can

2010 PORSCHE 918 SPYDER

Engine: Gasoline-fuelled V8 engine, with three electric motors on front and rear axles, plug-in hybrid

Displacement: 3397cc

Output: 350 horsepower (257kW) at 5700rpm

Gearbox: 7-speed PDK semi-automatic

Chassis: Carbon-fiber composite two-seat spyder monocoque with mid-engine

Performance: Maximum speed 200+ mph

lap the famed Nürburgring Nordschleife in less than 7 minutes 30 seconds, so its sporting credentials are not in doubt.

The driver controls the powertrain from the steering wheel. There are 4 different modes: E-Drive (full electric); Hybrid (where the gasoline engine can be used depending on street conditions for best fuel use); Sport Hybrid (with the power delivery more performance oriented); and Race Hybrid (using all the power for performance).

The Spyder emits less than 70 g/km CO_2 (to a European standard), equivalent to a fuel consumption of around 65 miles to each U.S. gallon (3l/100km or 78.4 miles/ imperial gallon).

The 918 Spyder underlines the critical requirement that for any sports car to succeed, it must look fantastic. From any angle, everybody who has seen the hybrid machine agrees it is one of the most attractive cars Porsche has ever built. It may be early days yet in terms of electric power, but this car ticked all the boxes in terms of conventional looks and performance. It was almost inevitable that a limited production series would follow, and in March 2011 a factory price of 645,000 Euros (excluding in-country taxes, etc.) for the 918 examples was announced, with deliveries starting November 2013. *Photos courtesy Porsche AG*

Did You Know?

The 918 Spyder was Porsche's first hybrid sports car concept model presented at the 2010 Geneva auto show. For light weight, the batteries are similar in technology to those used in mobile phones.

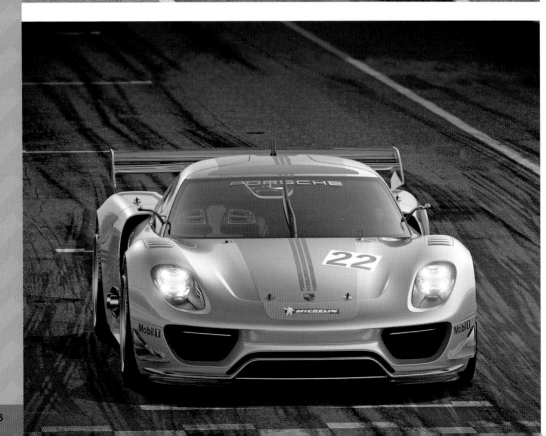

The GT3R hybrid made its debut in March 2010 and signified Porsche's intention to demonstrate its commitment to low emissions drivetrain technology in racing. However, the system used in the GT3 is unlike that used in the street hybrids. In the racer, two electric motors each provide an extra 81 horsepower (60kW) to the front wheels to supplement the car's regular 4-liter 480-horsepower flat-6. Instead of the batteries that are used in the street cars, the racer gets its electric power from a large flywheel generator mounted alongside the driver in the cabin. The system is charged

2010 PORSCHE GT3R HYBRID

Engine: Liquid-cooled flat 6-cylinder driving rear wheels, two permanently excited, water-cooled electric motors driving front wheels. Oil cooled flywheel-type electric storage unit

Displacement: 3996cc

Output: 480 horsepower at 7250rpm gasoline engine, 2 x 82 horsepower at 15,000rpm electric motors

Gearbox: 6-speed sequential, manual

Chassis: Unitary construction steel bodyshell with add-on carbon/Kevlar parts

Performance: Not available

whenever the driver uses the brakes—the two electric motors become generators and pass current to spin the storage flywheel at speeds up to 40,000 rpm. When the driver wants the extra power—for instance, leaving a corner—the flywheel passes its stored rotational energy to drive the two electric motors for 6–8 seconds (and so slowing the flywheel electro-magnetically). Unlike many street cars, it is the driver that selects when to use the electric power. The energy previously converted into heat whenever the brakes are used is therefore—in part—converted by the electrical generators into extra drive power. This is a similar arrangement to the Kinetic Energy Recovery Systems (KERS) used in Formula 1 racing. Porsche used an adapted flywheel storage system from the Williams F1 team's KERS units for the GT3R. The Williams system was unique in F1 for using the flywheel principle rather than the short-lived (and difficult to recycle) Lithium Ion batteries.

Did You Know?

On the face of it, a KERS-type hybrid system is far more environmentally acceptable than one using short-lived batteries. Nonetheless, Porsche appears to be hedging its bets as the technology evolves by developing all the current solutions.

The hybrid power system is used not only to provide extra power, but also to reduce overall fuel consumption, reducing fuel tank size (and the number of pit stops) required in a long-distance race. Porsche openly admitted at the car's public launch that the GT3R hybrid was a racing laboratory. Its performances in 2010 were limited and restricted by regulation, but in 2011, a GT3R hybrid finished the 24 Hours of Nürburgring well, and led the race in its early stages. Run on the old Nordschleife, this was a remarkable achievement given the standard of the competition and that the technology is still in its infancy. At the time of this writing, there is clearly much more to come from this system and rumors persist that a KERS-type hybrid will appear among the street 911 models. *Photos courtesy Porsche AG*

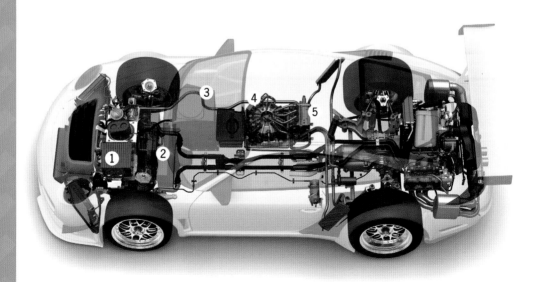

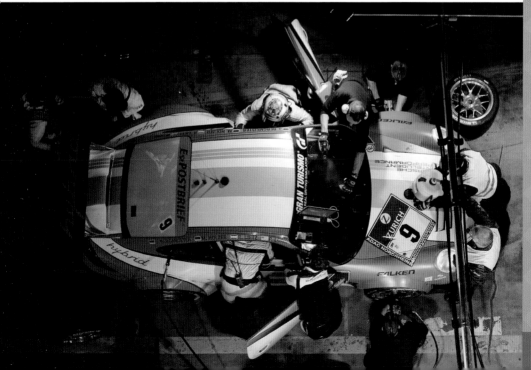

At the Frankfurt, Germany, auto show in September 2011, Porsche pulled the wraps off yet another new version of the 911. This was the all-new Type 991 model that would celebrate this evergreen sports car's 50th birthday in 2013.

The 991 is important because it represents a complete redesign of the car over the previous 997 model. It hardly needed to be said that the new car was instantly recognizable as a 911, and featured the unmistakable design cues that now make up the 911 design philosophy.

2012 911 CARRERA S (991)

Engine: Liquid-cooled 6-cylinder, double overhead camshafts, 4 valves per cylinder

Displacement: 3800cc

Output: 400 horsepower (294kW) at 7400rpm

Gearbox: 7 speed manual or 7-speed PDK automatic

Chassis: Rear engine, rear wheel drive, unitary construction steel 2+2 bodyshell

Performance: Maximum speed: 189 mph; 0–62mph in 4.3 seconds (with PDK)

Recalling earlier classic 911s, the headlamps were smaller and the exterior mirrors were mounted off the doors, rather than fitted to the window frames. The wheelbase was 3.9 inches (100 mm) longer, with a wider front track than the 997, and the roofline is lower. The overall effect made for a squatter appearance all around.

The 350 horsepower, direct fuel injection, 3.4-liter engine in the Carrera is up 5 horsepower from the 997 Gen 2 model, but has 16% less fuel consumption, and it even has the same reduction in emissions to just 194g/km (to a standard European cycle).

The 991 is up to 100 lbs (45 kg) lighter than the 997 through the use of aluminum and steel for the stiffer bodyshell. Combined with an improved aerodynamic profile (including a wider extending rear spoiler), combined cycle fuel use for the Carrera is claimed to be just under 31 miles to the U.S. gallon (8.5 l/100km). The ever popular S model develops an incredible 400 horsepower (up 15 horsepower) from its 3.8-liter flat-6 (an evolution of the 997 Gen 2 DFI powerplant).

The interior took its lead from the 2003 Carrera GT, with a high center tunnel and shift lever placed close to the steering wheel. The classic 5 round dials are kept, with one now being a multifunction display. The sophistication of the electronics is inevitably a most impressive part of the new model. On the "S" a new feature is Porsche Dynamic Chassis Control, which actively controls and stabilizes body roll when cornering.

We can be sure that the 991 will continue the long line that began back in 1963 with the 901. Back then, few would have dreamed that the quirky, rear-engined sports car would mature into a super-refined thoroughbred and still be with us 50 years later. *Photos courtesy Porsche AG*

Did You Know?
The 991 is only the third full redesign of the 911 since the 1963 original (the other being the 996 water-cooled model launched in 1997).

INDEX